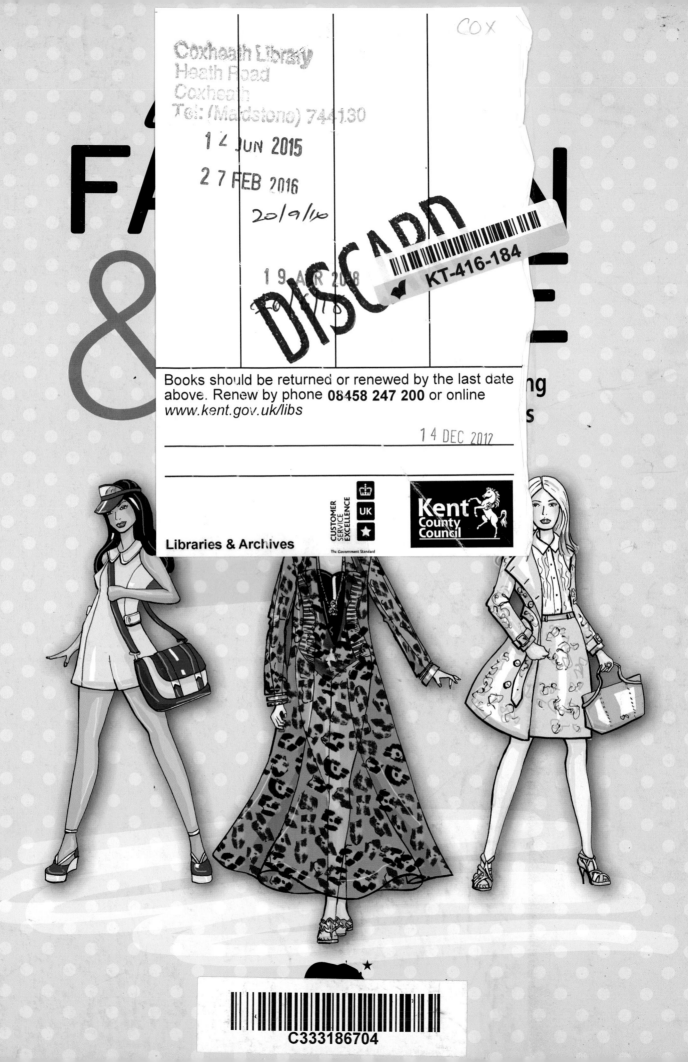

ARCTURUS

This edition published in 2012 by Arcturus Publishing Limited
26/27 Bickels Yard, 151–153 Bermondsey Street,
London SE1 3HA

ISBN: 978-1-84858-060-2
CH002174EN
Supplier 05, Date 0812, Print run 1561

Written and illustrated by Hilary Lovell
Designed by Dynamo Limited
Edited by Anna Brett

Printed in Singapore

CONTENTS

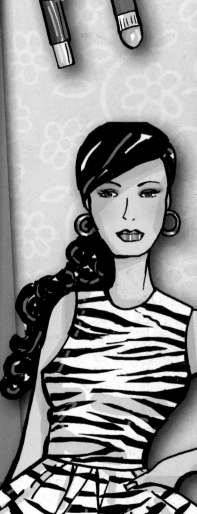

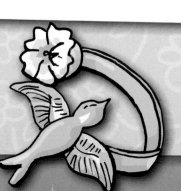

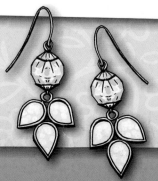

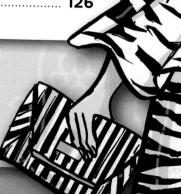

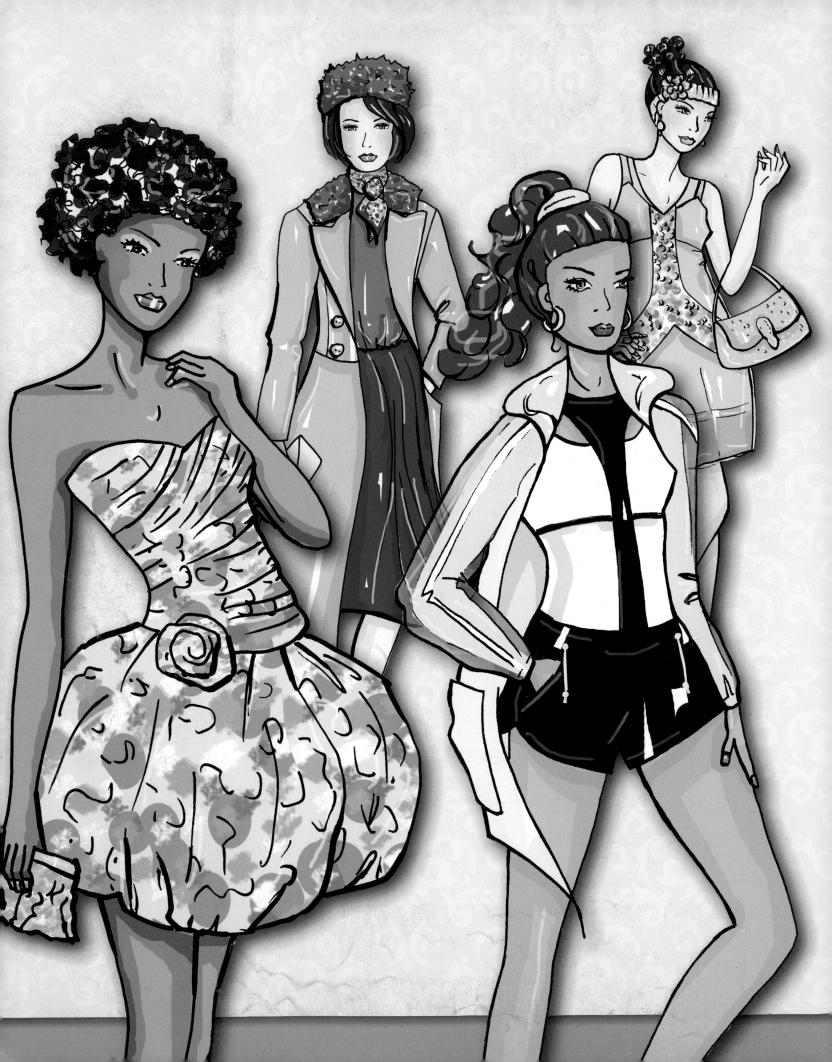

INTRODUCTION

Have you ever wondered how designers come up with new looks each season or fancied trying to design a collection of your own? This book is designed to help you do just that. Fashion designer Hilary Lovell breaks down styles from both the catwalk and design icons into clear, easy-to-follow steps.

Before you begin creating your collection, make sure you read the useful hints and tips in the opening section and the style cards at the end of each section. They will give you all the help you need to craft your own couture including the best use of accessories and fabric.

It's everything a future stylist needs to get going!

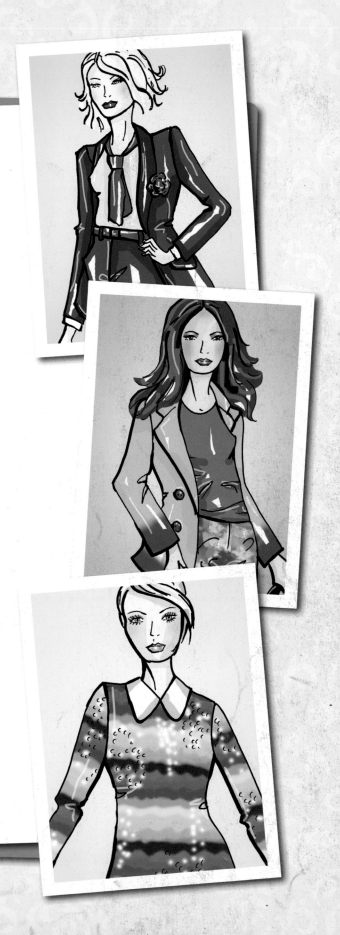

DRAWING TOOLS

Let's start by looking at the tools you'll need to create your fashion designs. It's a good idea to invest in the essentials, then build up your collection of drawing tools over time.

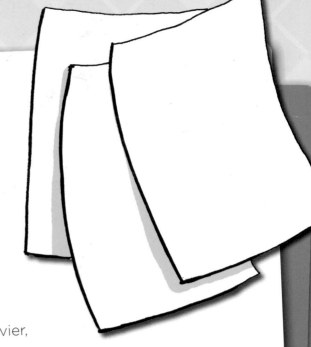

LAYOUT PAPER

There are so many different types of paper that it can seem difficult to know which is best for your drawings. It's a good idea to start with a basic, inexpensive paper such as layout paper while you experiment with the different features of your characters. When you have something you are happy with, you can move on to a heavier, higher-quality paper for your final version.

WATERCOLOUR PAPER

This type of paper is useful if you plan to colour your finished drawings using water-based paints. It is made from 100 per cent cotton and comes in a variety of weights and textures – 300 gsm (grams per square metre) or above is best.

CARTRIDGE PAPER

This top-quality paper is most frequently used for illustration and drawing, and is ideal for your final version. You don't need to buy the most expensive brand to get great results.

PENCILS

Most of your work will be done in pencil, so it's a good idea to make sure you are comfortable with the type of pencil you choose. Graphite, or lead, pencils come in different grades and are marked 'B' for blackness, or 'H' for hardness. '2H' is a good pencil to start with, as it leaves clean lines and few smudges. From here you can experiment with slightly blacker, or harder, pencils until you find one you are happy with. A lead holder pencil, or technical pencil, is useful because you can draw thinner lines with this, and the lead breaks less often than with a traditional pencil.

ERASER

Erasers come in three types: rubber, plastic and putty. All three can be effective, but most people start with rubber erasers.

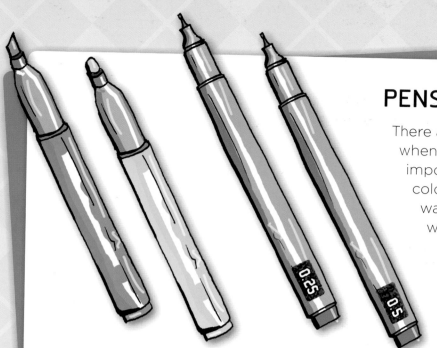

PENS

There are certain things to consider when choosing your ink pen. The most important of these is how you plan to colour your art. If you intend to use water-based paints, then you need a waterproof ink pen.

The nib thickness of most pens is marked on the lid, and usually ranges from 01 to 05. Nib thicknesses 02 or 03 are usually the best to work with. 01 is very fine, and best suited for inking tiny details on your model's outfit or face.

BRUSHES

Another way to ink your work is with a fine brush. This technique is quite difficult to master as it requires a very steady hand, and a good-quality sable brush. Brushes are great for adding glitter or sparkle details.

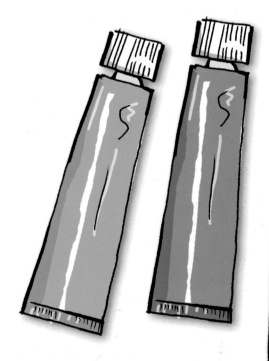

PAINTS

Most art stores stock a variety of paints including: acrylics, watercolours, oils and gouache. If you want to colour your characters by hand, it is best to experiment with different paints until you find one you are comfortable with.

COMPUTER

Another option is to scan your inked illustrations and then colour them digitally. Software programmes that let you create layers are useful for building depth into your illustrations.

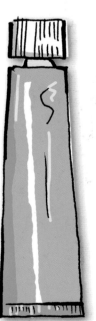

DRAWING TIPS

How to create your model

For fashion illustrations, it's useful to learn the basics of drawing the human form. Flicking though a fashion magazine or just looking in the mirror will give you an idea of the body's structure.

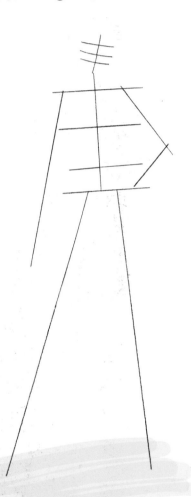

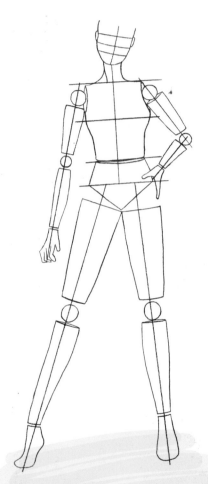

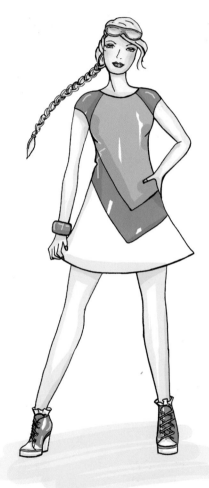

STEP 1

Start by drawing the basic frame of the body and the position for the facial features.

STEP 2

Build up your frame by using basic shapes such as cylinders for the arms and legs. Use balls for the shoulder, elbow and knee joints, and a simple body shape for the torso.

STEP 3

When you are happy with your pencil drawing, it's time to bring your model to life by adding fine details, followed by ink and final colour.

Elongating your model

One of the secrets of fashion drawing is knowing how to elongate your model. With longer legs, arms and neck, the model looks elegant and shows off the clothes to their best advantage.

▼ STANDARD BODY

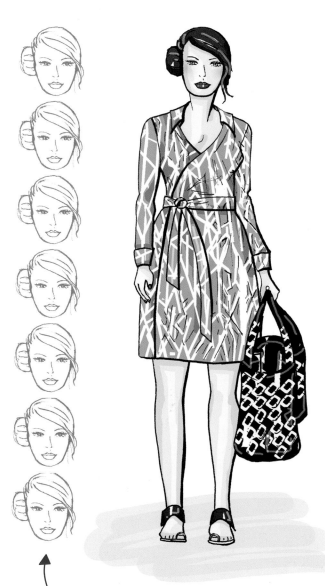

Standard body is the same height as 7 heads.

▼ ELONGATED MODEL

Elongate the neck, torso, arms and legs.

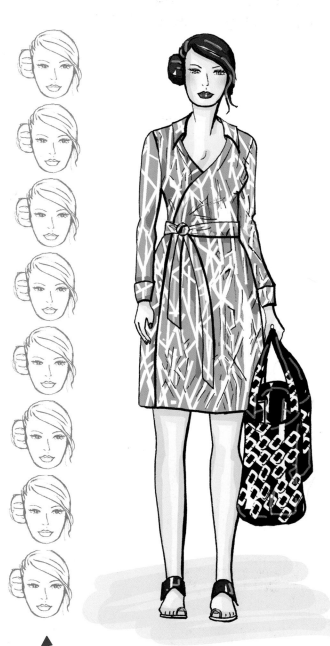

Elongated model pose is the same height as 8 heads.

INKING TIPS

Don't worry if your pencil drawings are a bit messy and smudged to start with — sketching and building your figure can involve a lot of corrections! When your model is complete and you are happy with the drawing, it's time to start inking.

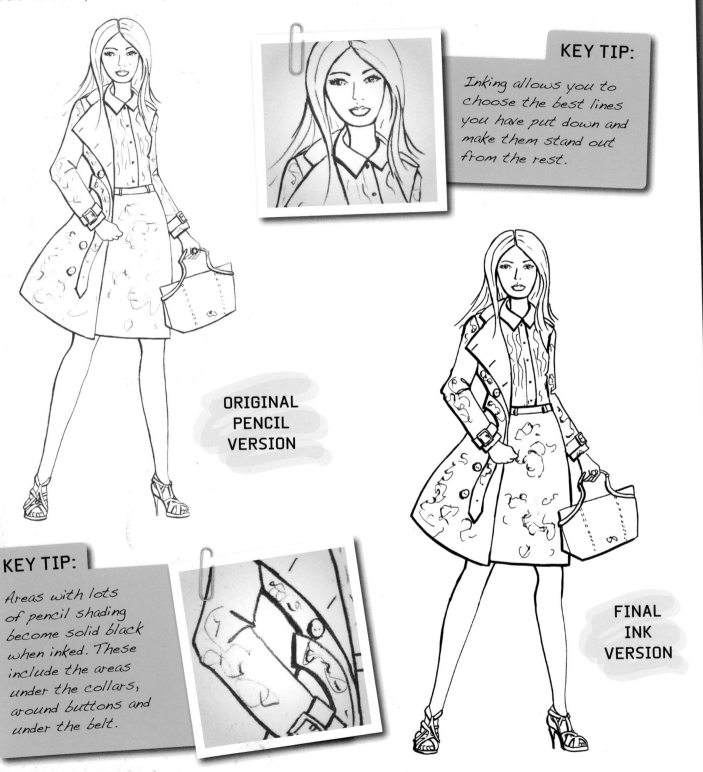

KEY TIP:

Inking allows you to choose the best lines you have put down and make them stand out from the rest.

ORIGINAL
PENCIL
VERSION

KEY TIP:

Areas with lots of pencil shading become solid black when inked. These include the areas under the collars, around buttons and under the belt.

FINAL
INK
VERSION

COLOURING TIPS

After the inking stage, it's time to colour your model. Start by applying your base tones, then build up the colour by layering other shades on top. Experiment with pens, pencils and paints until you achieve the desired result.

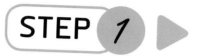 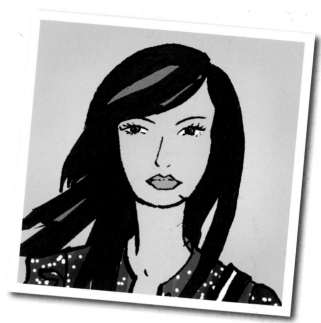

Start by deciding on your colour scheme, then lay down your basic tones.

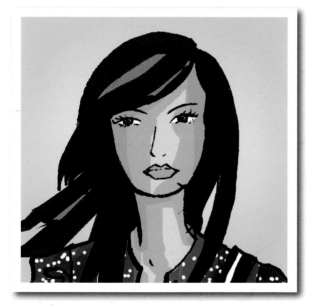 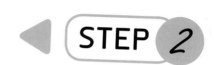

Next, using darker tones of the base colours, add the shaded areas to your model.

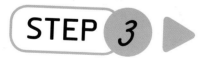 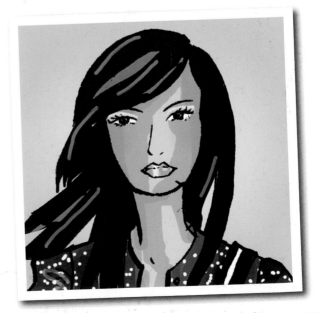

Finally, add highlights to the areas where light would reflect, using whites and lighter shades of the base colours. Highlights to eyeshadow and lipstick give the make up a glossy finish.

DRAWING PATTERNS AND PRINTS

Creating a three-dimensional appearance on paper can be quite difficult. Here we give you some tips to make your paper take on the texture of soft flowers, shiny sequins, animal print and distinct designer fabrics.

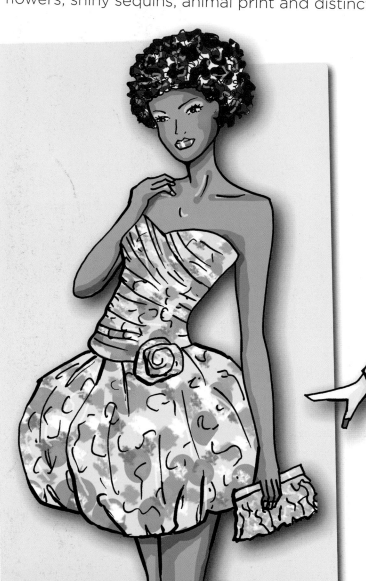

FLORAL PRINTS:

The best way to create a floral print for your outfit is to start off by putting in your base colour. Over the top of the base, add rounded patches of your next colour choice. Then, add smaller patches of colour for your flowers, placing them evenly over the print to create a floral effect.

SHINY PRINTS:

To give a garment a shiny print, start by colouring up your garment to your chosen look. Over the top of this, add white highlights in clusters where you would imagine the light would catch the fabric. For instance on the shoulders, hip area and skirt.

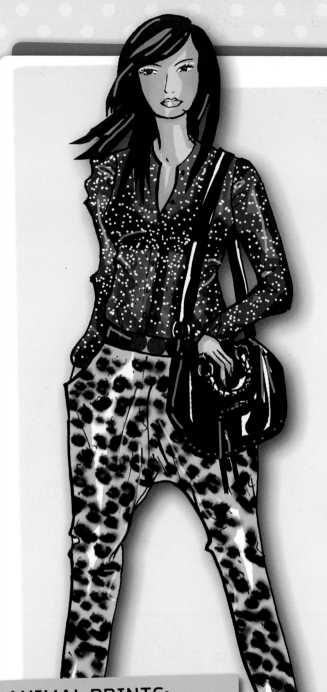

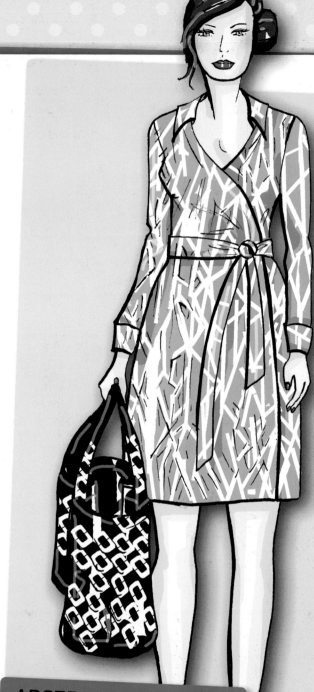

ANIMAL PRINTS:

To create mixed animal print, add your base colours first then work up the print over the top. Use shading on the base colour where required, to give more shape to the outfit. When using multiple prints in your design, apply the boldest print to what you want to be the main feature. Use smaller prints on the other items to complement the feature garment.

ABSTRACT PRINTS:

To create an abstract fabric print, begin by working up your base colour using shading around the body to give the garment shape. Next, work over the top of the base colour. If the print is white it is a good idea to leave a few large highlights on your base colour, which will work to soften a busy print.

PRETTY ROMANTIC

The modern princess can feel extra dreamy in lovely lace, floral fabrics and pretty pastels. Go all soft and sweet and create your own fashion fairy tale.

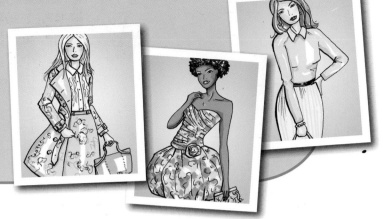

Lace Coat and Skirt

SMART DAY

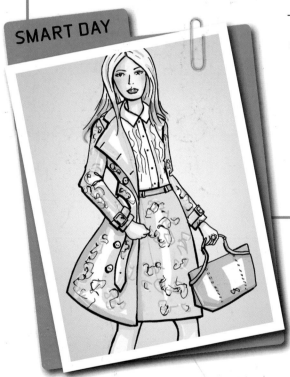

This is a modern, classy way to use lace in a gorgeous day outfit. It looks great with strappy sandals and is brought bang up to date with dip-dye hair.

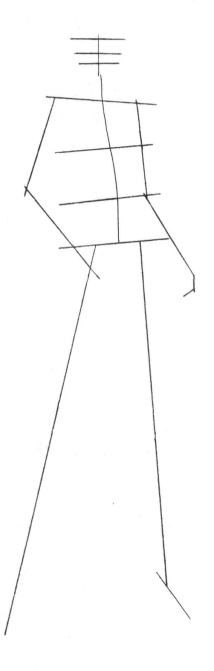

1 Create your pose with your frame, using clear lines to map out the figure.

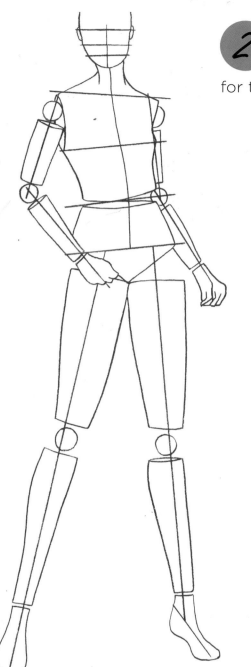

2 Fill out the frame by drawing the body shape, using cylinders and balls for the limbs and joints.

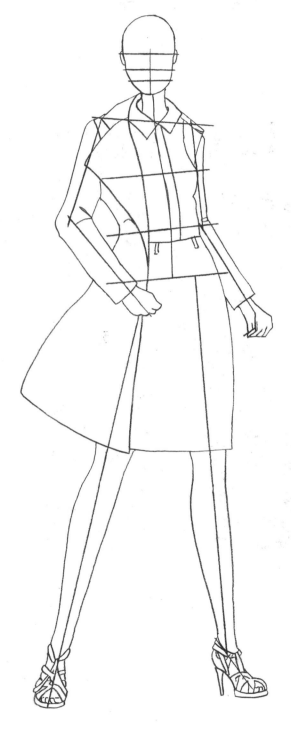

3 Start drawing the outfit in over the top of your body shape. Flare out the coat so that you can see more of it to help show off the lace detail. Add the strappy sandals at this point too.

4 Remove the frame lines and draw in the hairstyle and facial features. Add buttons to the coat and shirt, and the belt and cuff details to the tailored coat.

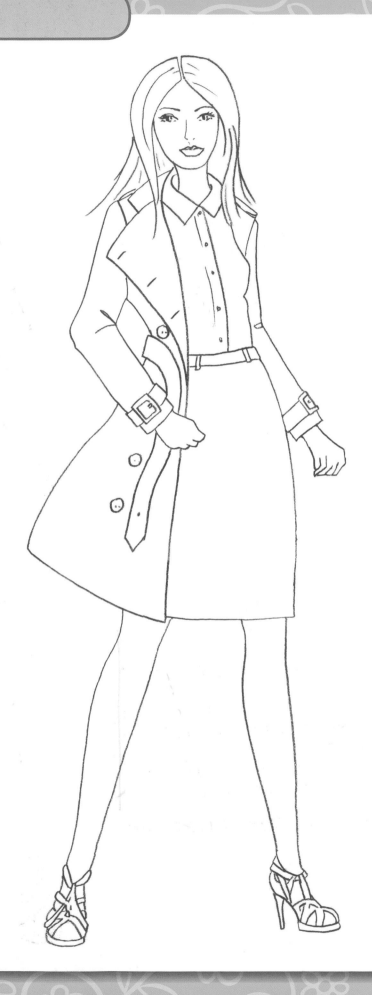

5 Softly draw the lace detail on the jacket and the skirt. Light, curled lines, randomly spaced, will give the appearance of vintage lace. Add the ruffles to the front of the shirt.

Add an Accessory

Draw a simple handbag with a soft, stitched detail on the front. A feature ring works well on the hand holding the bag.

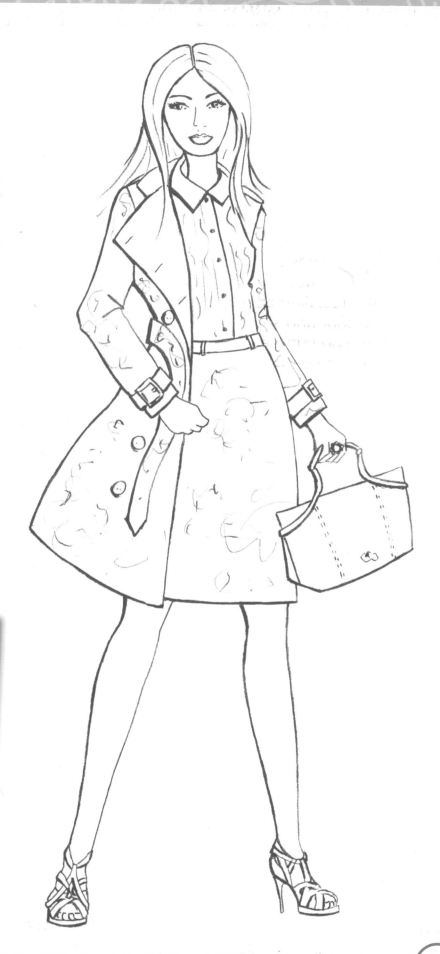

6 Now add the ink to your finished drawing. Use a thicker line around the bag, under the skirt and around the coat belt and buttons to make them stand out. Give the lace detail thin and thick lines to emphasize the fabric on the coat and skirt.

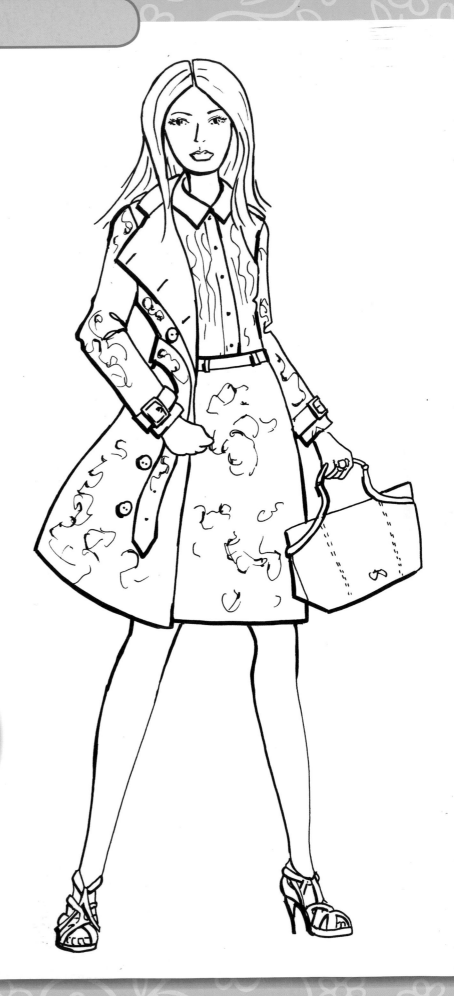

Stylist's tip

For the lace detail use a very quick squiggle with your pencil/ink. That way it looks a lot more freehand which is how fashion drawing should be.

7 Soft pink with lilac accessories works well with this outfit. Top the clothing off with a bright pink dip-dye on light blonde hair to make it really stand out against the coat.

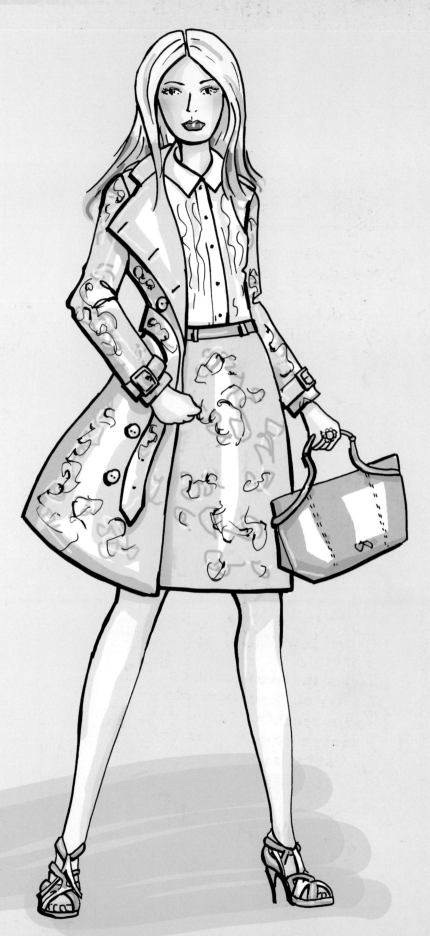

Floral Puffball Dress

This beautiful floral puffball dress is perfect for a first date or just a walk on a balmy night. It looks great accessorized with a ruffle clutch bag and love-heart kitten heels.

TRENDY EVENING

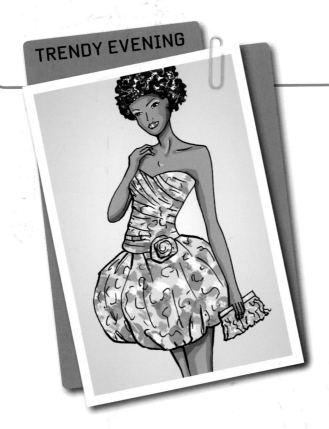

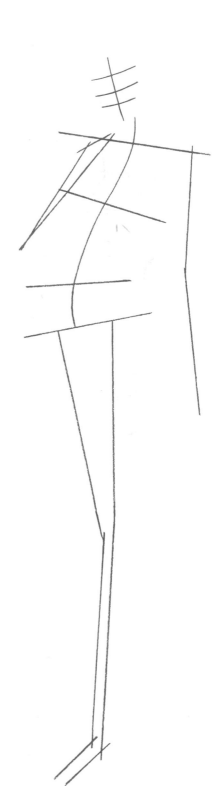

1 Start by drawing the frame of your model. To emphasize the body shape use a strong curve going up into the tilt of the head.

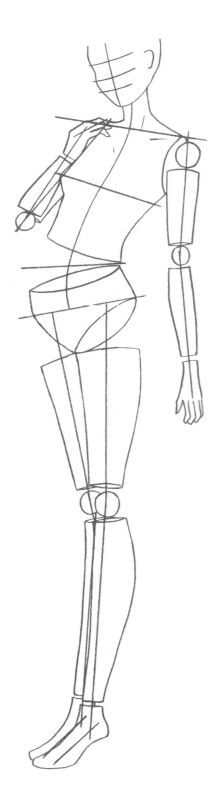

2 Work up the structure of the body, using cylinder shapes for the limbs and torso, and balls for the joints.

3 Draw in the lines of the outfit. The sweetheart neckline of the dress is emphasized by the gathered lines which sweep across the body. Puff out the skirt nice and big following the angle of the body. Add the heels with the love-heart detail.

4 Remove the frame lines and add a soft Afro hairstyle and facial features. Keeping the hair short makes a feature of the neckline of the dress.

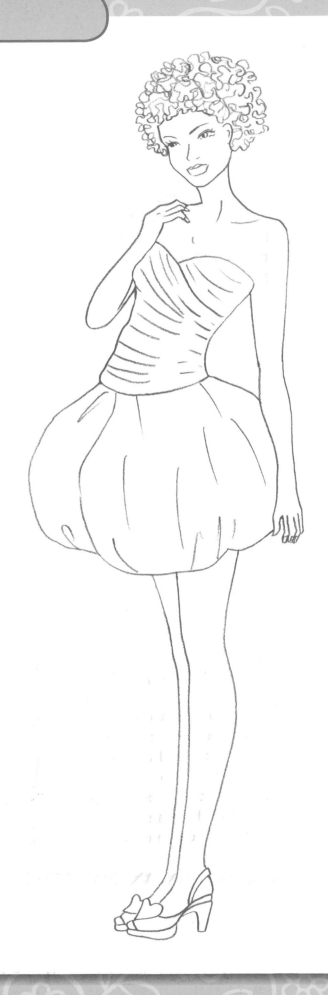

5 Add squiggly lines all over the dress for the floral print. Remember the round petal shapes should be evenly spread over your outfit.

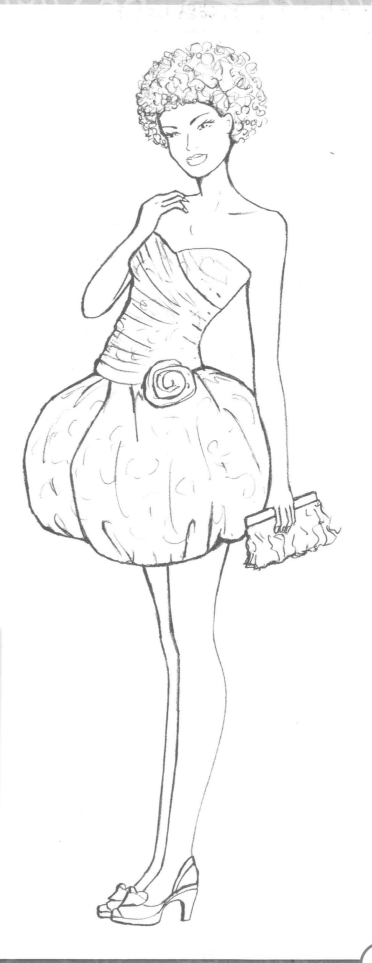

Add an Accessory

Very few accessories are required for this chic outfit. A ruffle clutch bag gives the outfit simple softness and the addition of a fabric flower at the waist draws the eye to the dress.

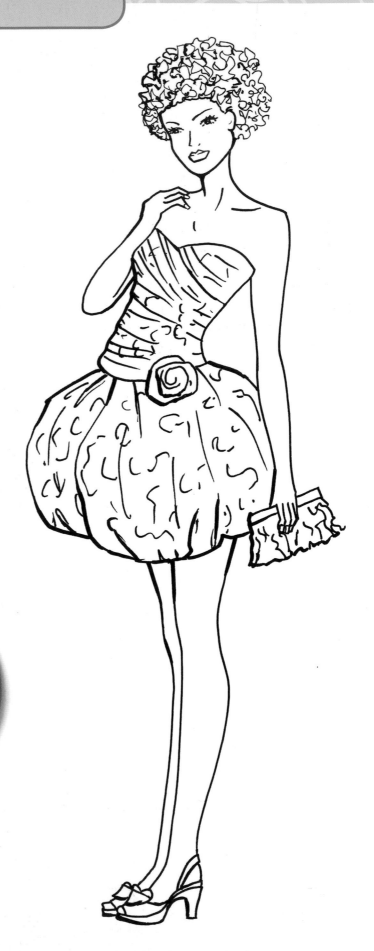

6 Now it is time to add your ink. Keep the thick lines for under the skirt and under the bag. Draw fast curved lines around the shape of the body and the skirt for the gathers. Give the flower thicker lines to really make it a feature.

Stylist's tip

Placing the right hand on the shoulder gives the pose a romantic feel which works well with this dress.

7 Yellow, peach, white and blue floral print really works well for this dress. Against the model's dark skin the dress has ultimate impact. It is enhanced by peach accessories and make up.

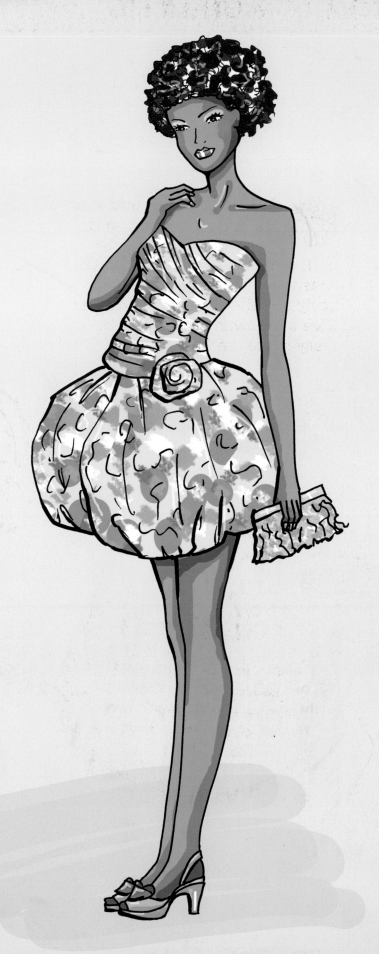

Pleated Maxi Skirt

This pretty outfit is long and chic with soft colours and details. The floor length skirt is perfect for the day and will definitely turn heads.

SMART CASUAL

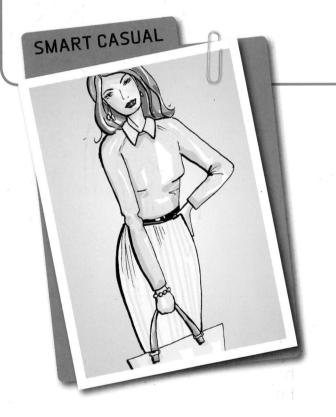

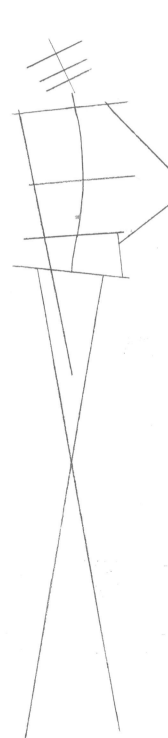

1 Start by drawing your frame for this relaxed pose with a curved body and tilted head.

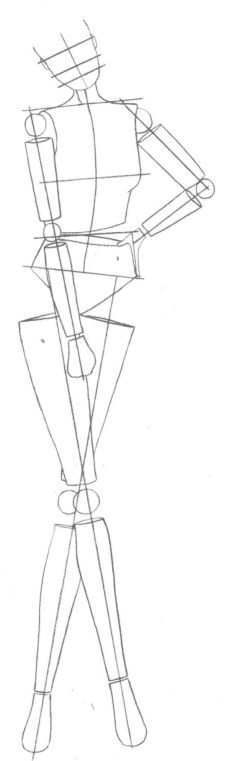

2 Draw in the cylinder shapes and balls for the joints to fill out the figure.

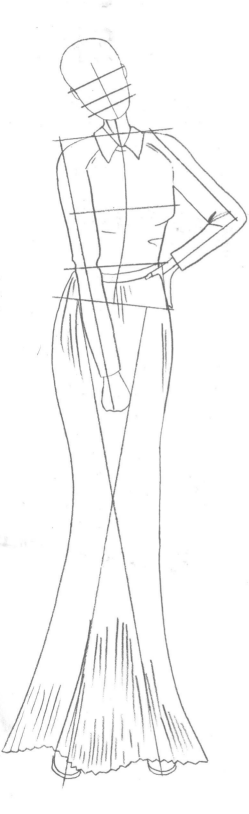

3 Now draw in the outfit, giving the skirt a simple silhouette from the hips and flaring it out at the ankles. Add the detail to the pleating and give the skirt a zig-zag hem.

4 Draw in the facial features and the hair. Keep the hairstyle soft and flowing. Follow the tilt of the head for the waves in the hair.

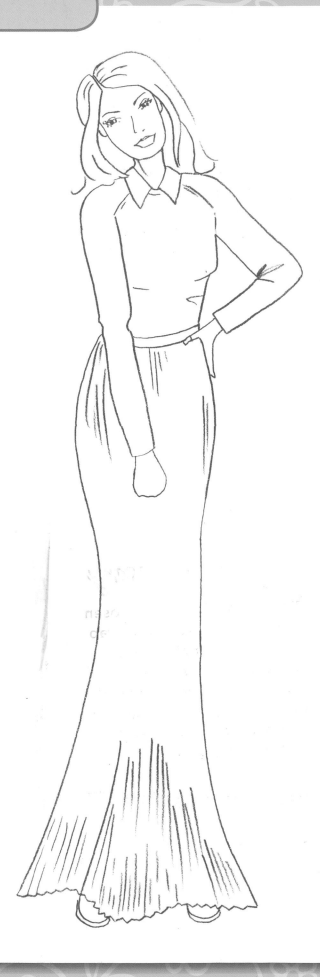

5 Make sure the pleat lines follow the shape of the skirt down the body. The hand held in front of the waist helps draw attention to the lines on the skirt.

Add an Accessory

For this outfit, we've chosen a pretty day bag with strap detail, a simple beaded bracelet and soft feather earrings. Having the head tilted keeps the earrings from being hidden by the hair, making them a feature.

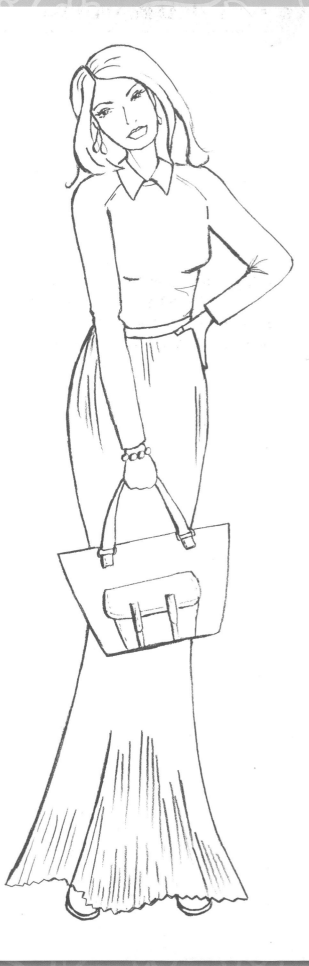

6 To work up your ink, use the thicker lines around the outside of the body, under the bag, around the collar and within the hair. The pleats on the skirt need to remain thin and soft.

Stylist's tip

Practise poses in the mirror to really see how the body shape works under the model's clothing so you get the perfect silhouette.

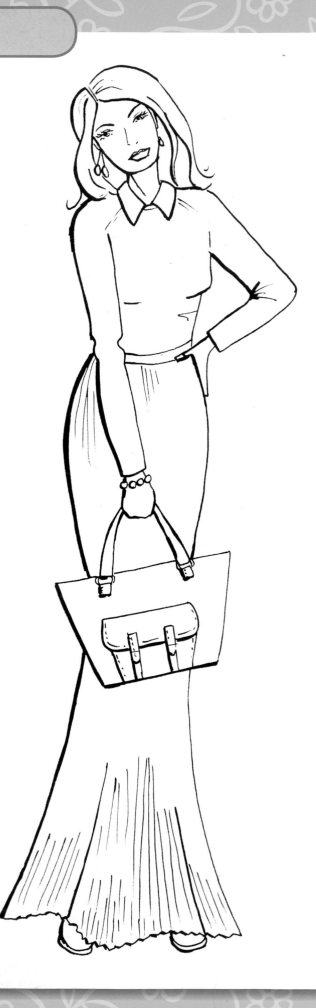

7 A pastel palette works well with this lovely soft, daytime outfit. The pink, peach and blue, with matching shoes and accessories, are enhanced by the black belt and the red hair of the model.

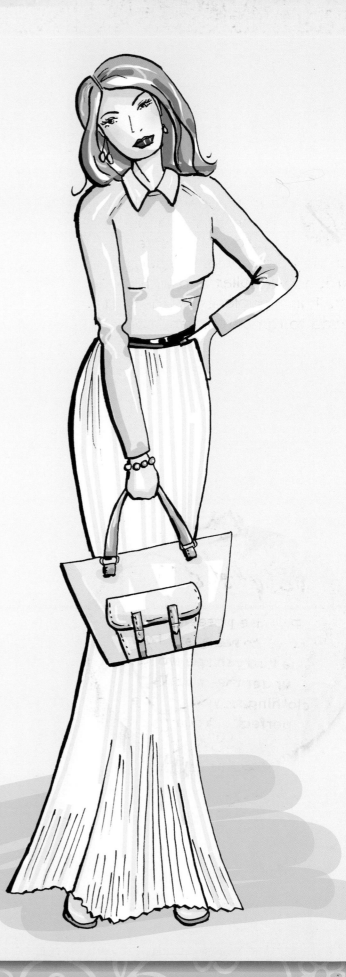

STYLE CARDS

For a pretty, romantic style the accessories need to have a gentle, delicate feel. Simple styles with an added feature of ruffles, lace or florals work well in soft pastel colours, dusty pinks and mauves.

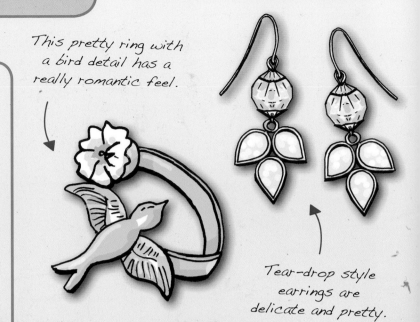

This pretty ring with a bird detail has a really romantic feel.

Tear-drop style earrings are delicate and pretty.

HAIR:

Whether sweeping the hair away from the face or leaving it loose, romantic hairstyles are enhanced with a pretty accessory or a simple hair band.

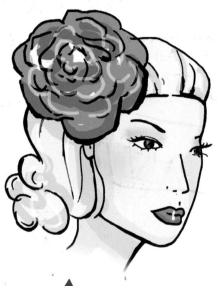

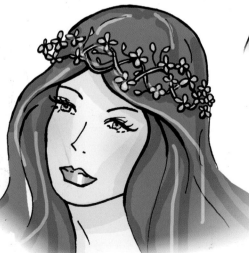

A top plait can look simple and stylish. Leave some strands loose for a relaxed feel.

A large soft flower accessory placed to one side will complement an outfit with a similar colour.

For a really special romantic look this delicate flower hair band is perfect. This will work best with long, wavy hair.

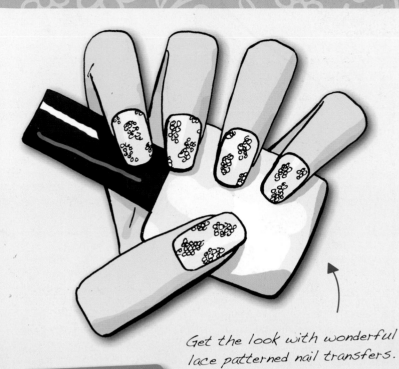

Get the look with wonderful lace patterned nail transfers.

BAGS:

Clutch bags are perfect to show off the intricate patterns of ruffles or lace.

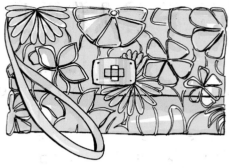

This lace bag will give any outfit a touch of femininity.

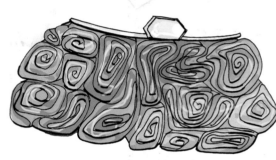

The ruffles on this bag can look like flowers... a perfect addition to a floral dress.

SHOES:

Getting the romantic look for evening or daytime is no problem with these shoe styles, both enhanced by ruffle features.

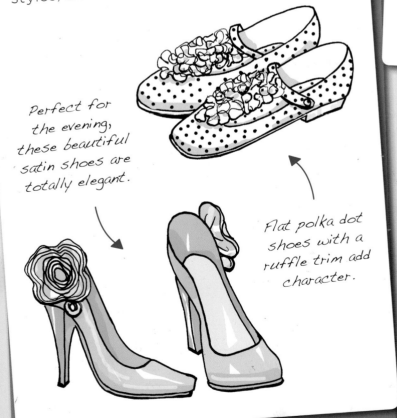

Perfect for the evening, these beautiful satin shoes are totally elegant.

Flat polka dot shoes with a ruffle trim add character.

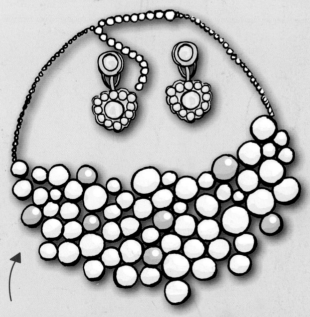

Finish off an outfit with pearls and beaded earrings.

ANIMAL PRINTS

For a hot summer look, take inspiration from the sun-drenched African plains. From zebra to leopard, animal prints will always be as natural as their muses.

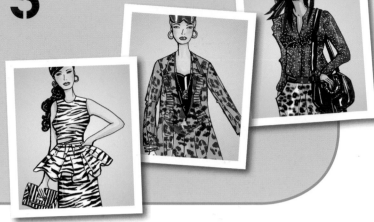

Zebra Peplum Dress

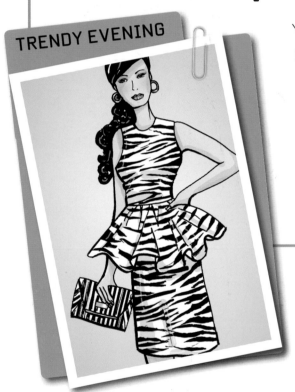

TRENDY EVENING

You cannot help being noticed in this zebra print dress. Bold, strong and exotic, this look is complete with the addition of daring black and white striped shoes and clutch bag.

1 Create your frame with straight lines, using a soft curve through the centre of the body.

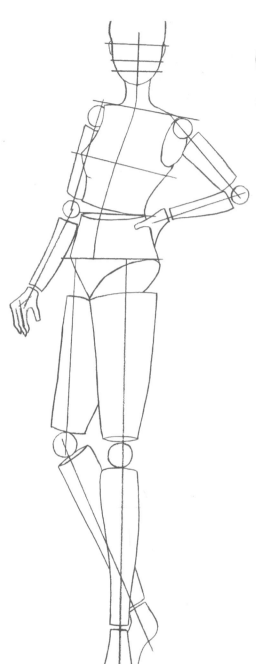

2 Add the shape of the body using the basic cylinder and ball shapes on the frame.

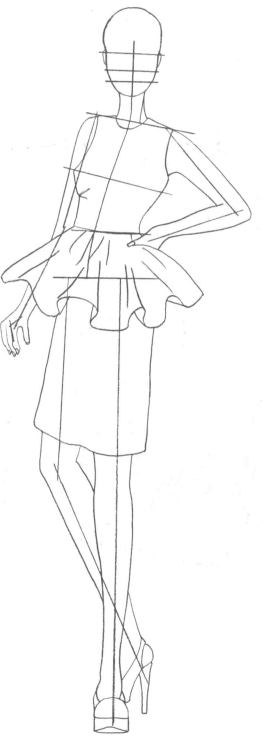

3 Create the outfit using clean lines. A ruffle peplum is added to the waist to give the dress an exciting shape. Very high-heeled shoes give the model an elegance that works well with the pose.

4 Add the features to the face and work up the hairstyle. A side ponytail with wild curls works well with the smooth side parting. The ruffle peplum is also enhanced by the curls.

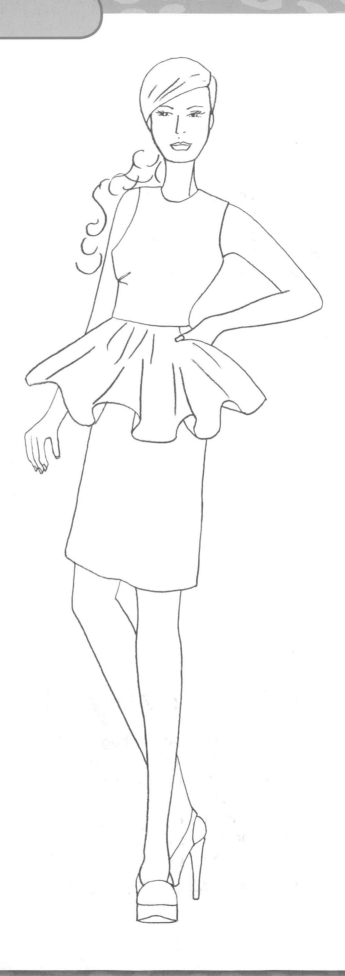

5 The zebra print detail is added to the dress in strong, dashed lines, all horizontal to get the best effect.

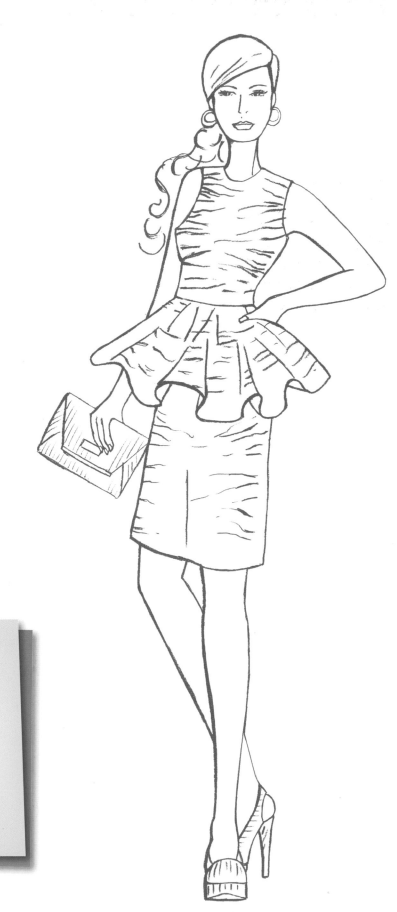

Add an Accessory

Add a striped clutch bag and matching stripes on the shoes. Very little jewellery is required for this outfit due to the fabric print, so a simple pair of hoop earrings is enough.

6 Start inking your pencil. Use thick lines which run thinner or disappear completely for the stripes on both the dress and accessories. Use the thicker lines under the ruffled skirt to make it really stand out against the print.

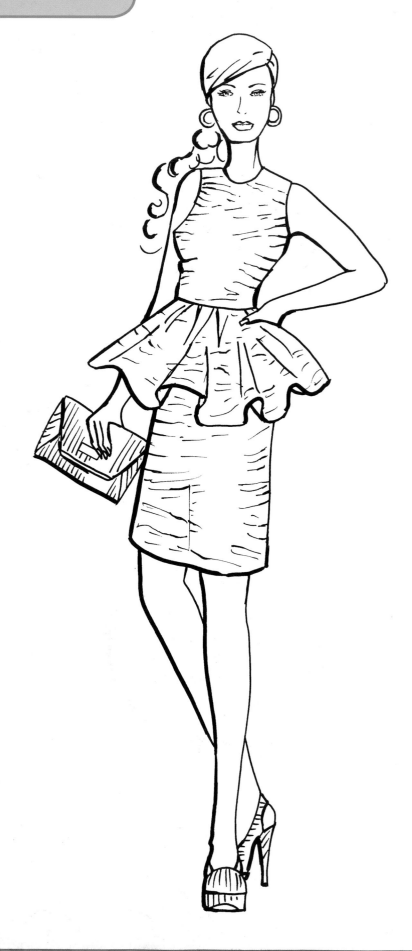

7 Now for the colour – pure black and white for the model to really make a statement. The hair is dark and the make up is subtle so the dress says it all.

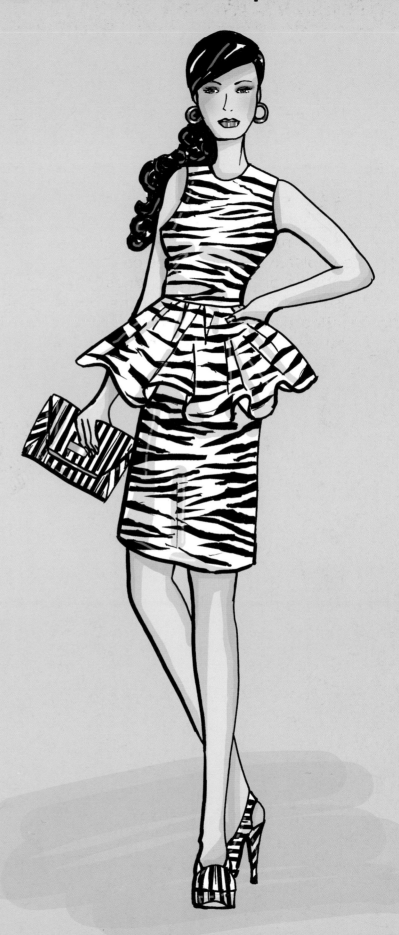

Stylist's tip

Adding a grey on the zebra print dress softens the contrast of the black and white and gives the dress shape.

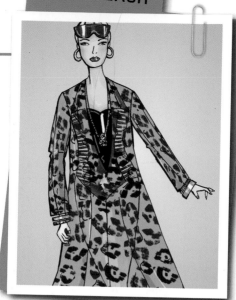

Leopard-print Kaftan

For the ultimate glamorous beach-style outfit, this kaftan has it all. Sheer leopard-print fabric with lots of movement and beautiful golden accessories needs to be worn with plenty of attitude.

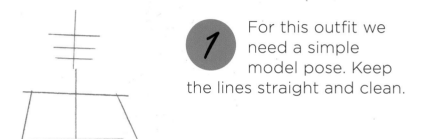

1 For this outfit we need a simple model pose. Keep the lines straight and clean.

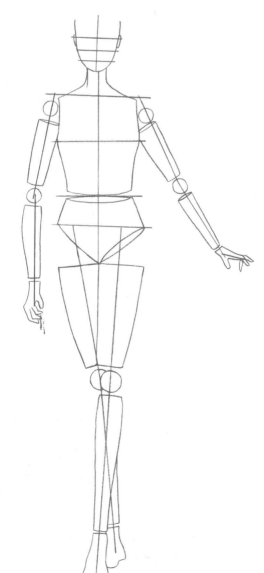

2 Add the ball shapes to the joints and cylinders for the limbs and torso.

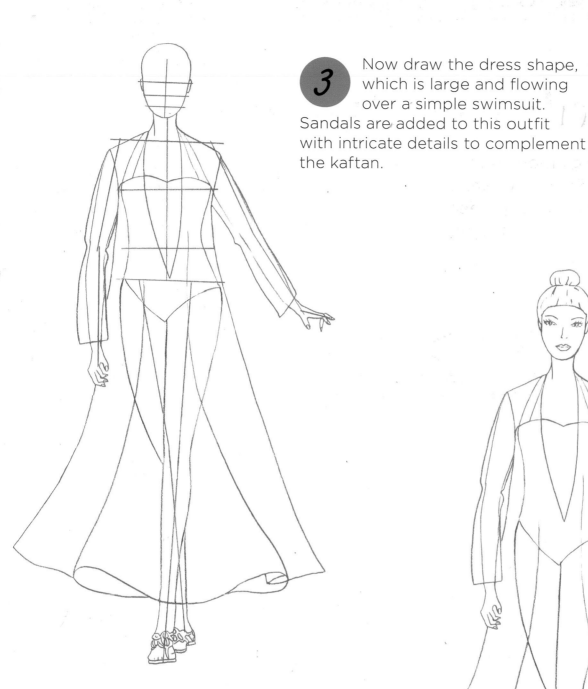

3 Now draw the dress shape, which is large and flowing over a simple swimsuit. Sandals are added to this outfit with intricate details to complement the kaftan.

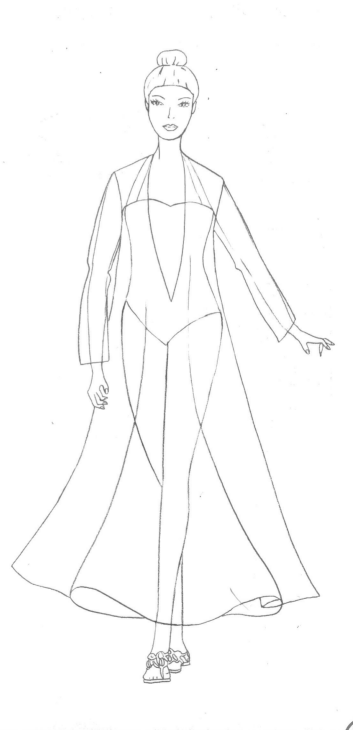

4 The hair and face details are now added. Keeping the hairstyle simple and swept up off the face in a high bun gives the feeling of height. It also helps enhance the shape of the kaftan from the shoulders, flowing down the arms.

5 Lovely summery jewellery is added to this model – chunky bangles, large hoop earrings and, of course, shades. Adding a long pendant necklace helps give focus to the feature V-neck on the kaftan. The swimsuit has stripes added to the sides to enhance the model's shape.

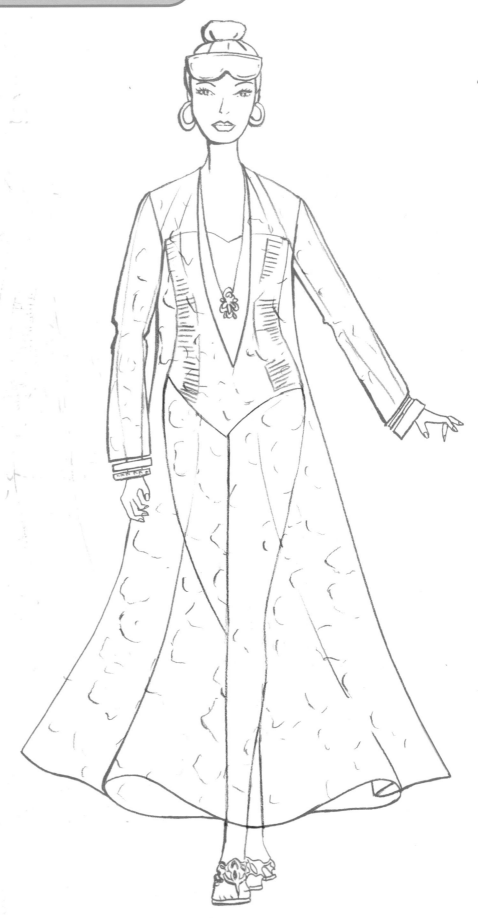

6 Time for the ink. Adding thicker lines around the base of the dress to show the fullness of the skirt really works well. Also, thicker lines around the jewellery and shades helps them stand out.

Stylist's tip

Having the arm gently out to the right enhances the movement of the soft, sheer fabric used for this kaftan.

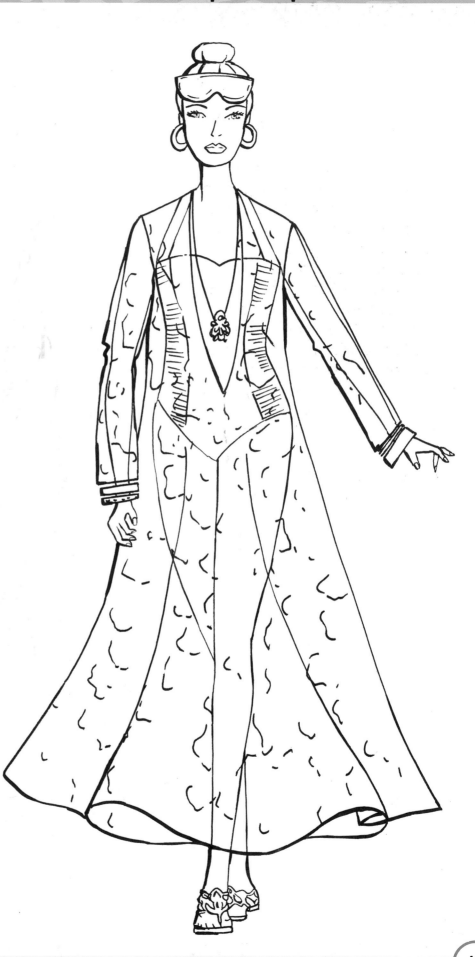

7 Soft browns are used for this leopard print, overlapping slightly in places to show the fullness of the fabric. Golds and bronzes are used for the jewellery, sandals and shades to keep the look soft against the black of the swimsuit. Finish off with sunny blonde hair.

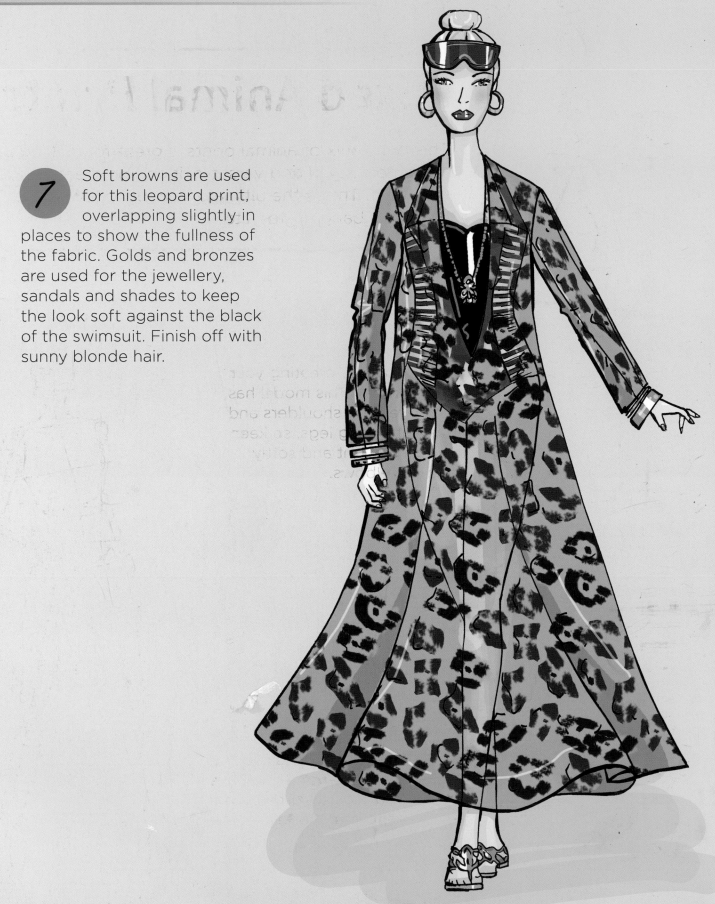

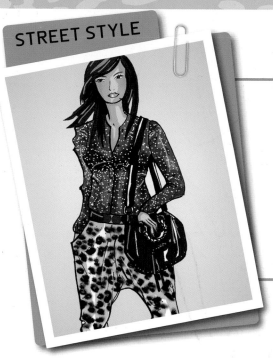

STREET STYLE

Mixed Animal Prints

This multi-mix of animal prints is great for making a statement. Bold and versatile, it can be dressed up or down. This is the ultimate girl-about-town look which is bang up to date.

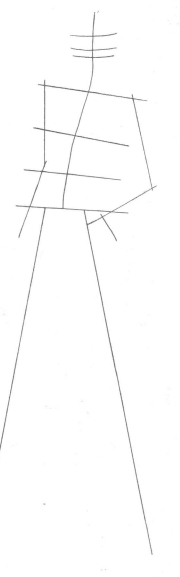

1 Start by creating your frame. This model has relaxed shoulders and arms but strong legs, so keep the legs straight and softly bend the elbows.

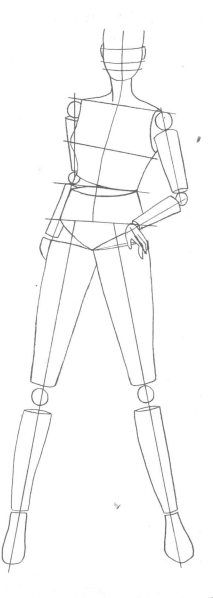

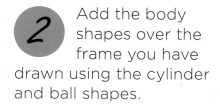

2 Add the body shapes over the frame you have drawn using the cylinder and ball shapes.

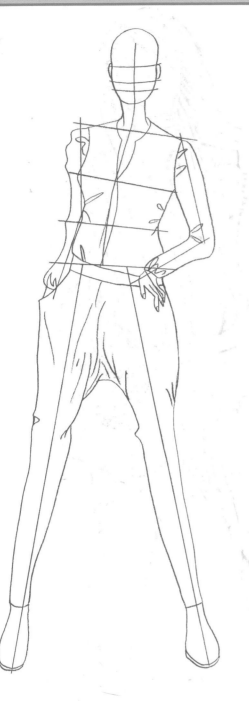

3 Over the body shape, draw in your clothing. Keep the lines soft and curved to show the creasing of the harem pants and shirt. Add simple boots.

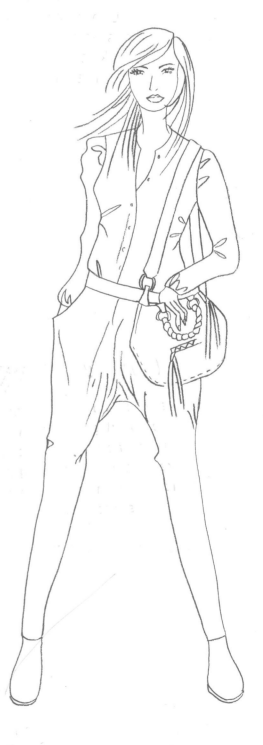

4 Now draw in your facial features and hairstyle. The hair is loose and by using curved lines going over the shoulder, it will give the model movement. Also draw in the button detail on the shirt.

5 At this stage, softly draw in the print detail for the shirt, trousers and shoes. Small dots and swirls will help you know where to ink and colour later.

Add an Accessory

Due to this outfit having lots of print going on, we keep the accessories to a bare minimum. Adding a handbag with tassel detail is enough.

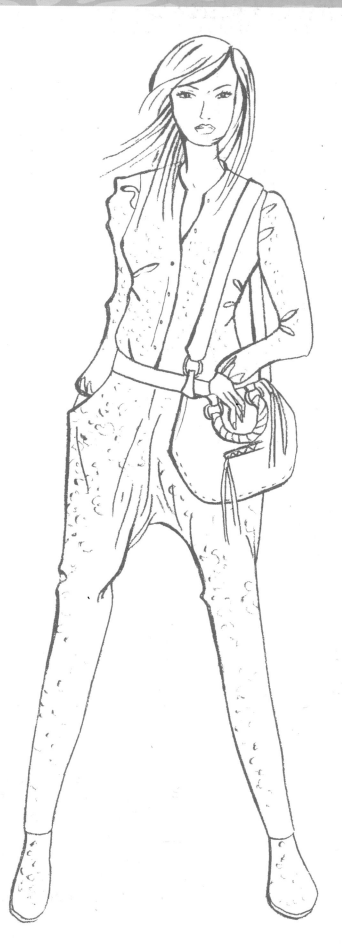

6 Over your finished pencil, start working with the ink. Use soft, thin, curved lines for the creasing on the clothing, tassels and hair. Then use thicker lines around the bag and shirt.

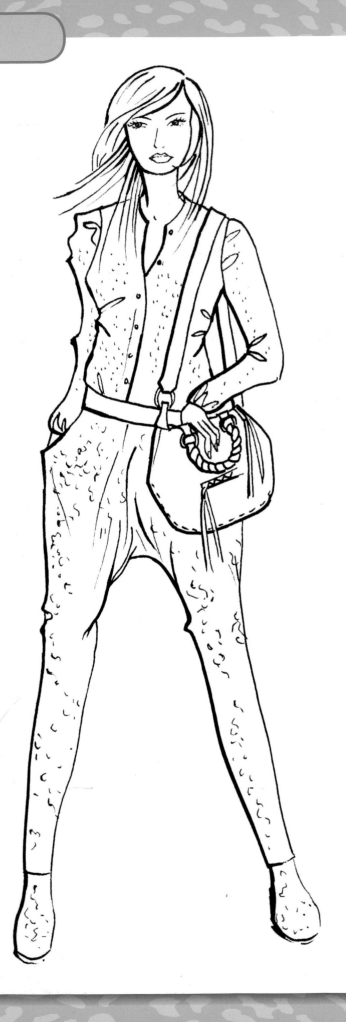

Stylist's tip

Drawing the fringe parting on the opposite side to where the hair is swishing away gives the model a relaxed feel.

7 Black, white and grey are mainly used on this outfit, with the exception of the tan leopard-print boots. Keep the shirt sheer and soft so you can see a subtle impression of the body underneath.

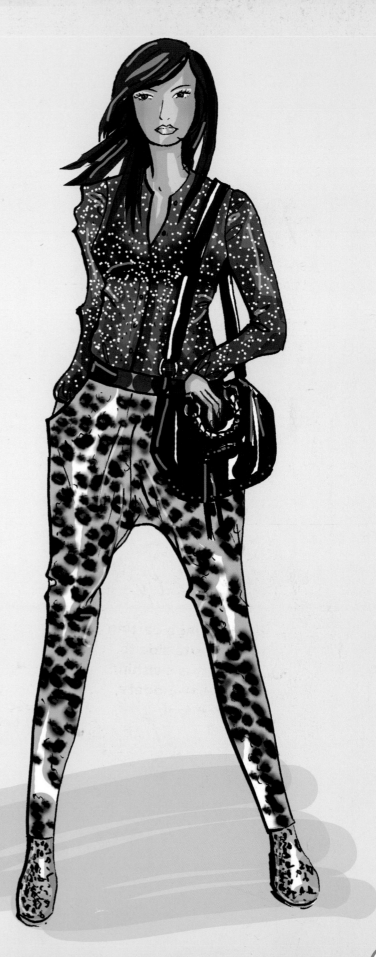

STYLE CARDS

You can find animal print on all sorts of accessories. Although care needs to be taken when putting them together on one outfit. This trend is great fun to experiment with.

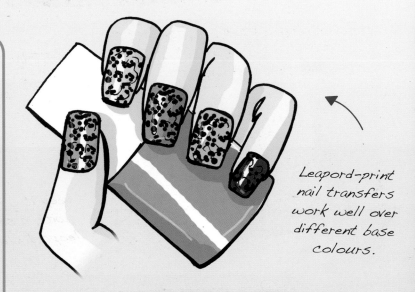

Leapord-print nail transfers work well over different base colours.

SHOES:

Whether working the animal print in killer heels or pumps, shoes are a great way to work the look.

Zebra print adds style to a pair of high-heels.

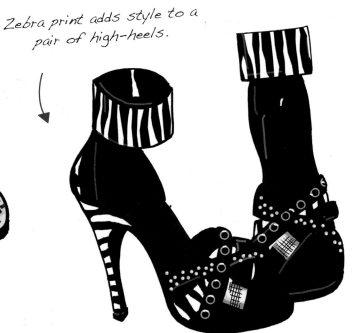

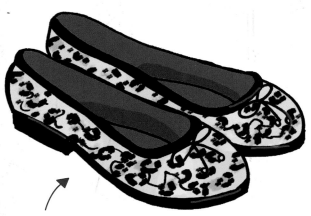

Perfect pumps enhance a daytime outfit.

Fun animal-print dress rings are ideal for making a statement.

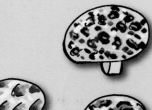
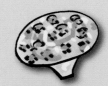

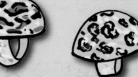

Add animal print into your hairstyle with these fun hair bands.

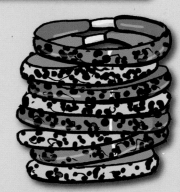

BAGS:

Animal-print bags, large or small, can make a statement and enhance a plain outfit in their own way.

Make a statement with this large zebra-print handbag.

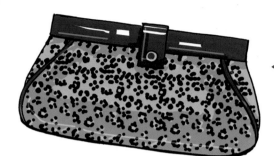

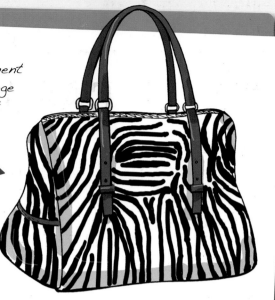

Keep it subtle with a small leopard clutch.

ACCESSORIES:

Animal print can be used on any accessory whether it is a hat, scarf or sunglasses – you need never be without it.

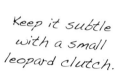

These sunglasses are perfect for summer animal-print style.

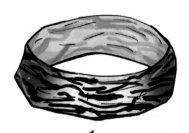

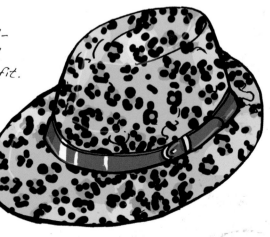

This large animal-print bangle will finish off any outfit.

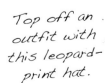

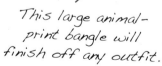

Top off an outfit with this leopard-print hat.

A sheer chiffon animal-print scarf is great for day or evening.

BOLD AND BRIGHT

Vibrant outfits and accessories are not for the faint-hearted. You can't be a wallflower with a neon skirt or a dazzling jacket – and with such stunning outfits, why would you want to be anything other than bright, bold and beautiful?

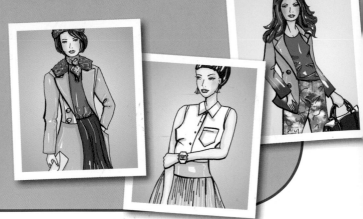

Stylish Colour Blocking

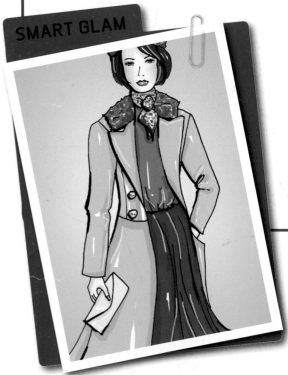

SMART GLAM

This lovely winter coat with faux fur trim and matching hat is placed over a wonderful, brightly coloured top and skirt for an exciting contrast and twist to the outfit. This proves that winter clothes don't have to be dull.

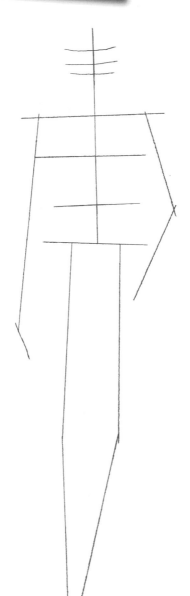

1 Create the frame of your model. For this relaxed pose, use straight lines with a gentle bend in the knee.

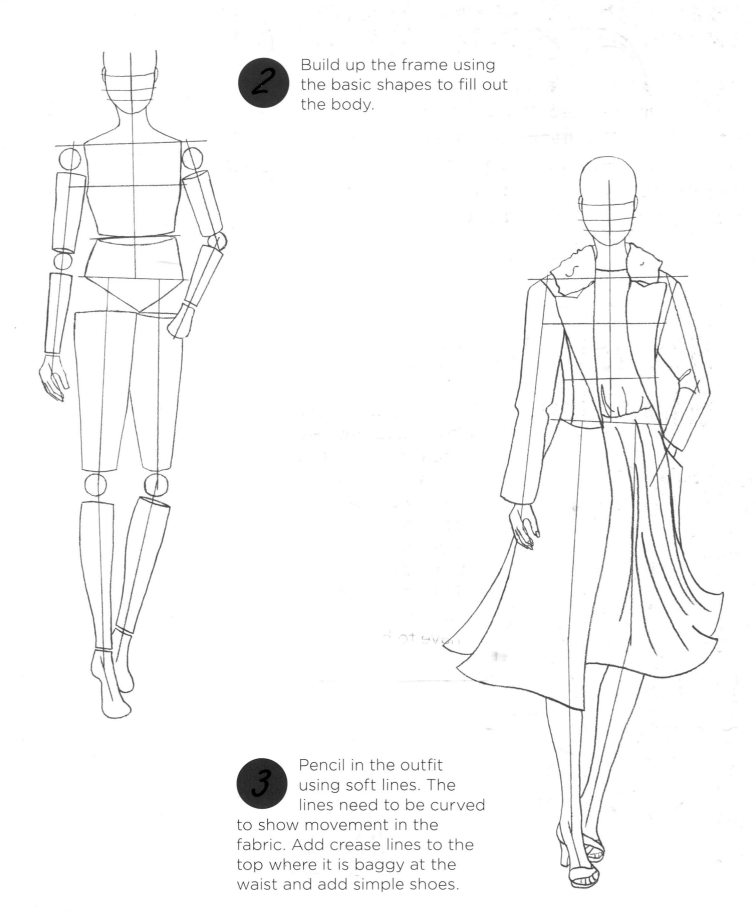

2 Build up the frame using the basic shapes to fill out the body.

3 Pencil in the outfit using soft lines. The lines need to be curved to show movement in the fabric. Add crease lines to the top where it is baggy at the waist and add simple shoes.

4 Add the facial features and the hair – the hairstyle is a simple bob, again using curved, soft lines to give it movement. Large buttons can to be added to the coat.

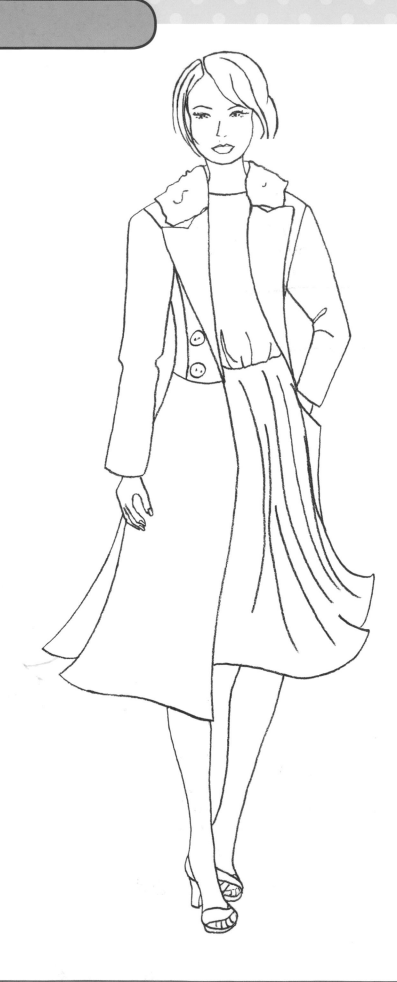

5 Now it's time to add the extra touches. A neck scarf is added to the outfit to enhance the faux fur collar and a simple clutch bag finishes it off.

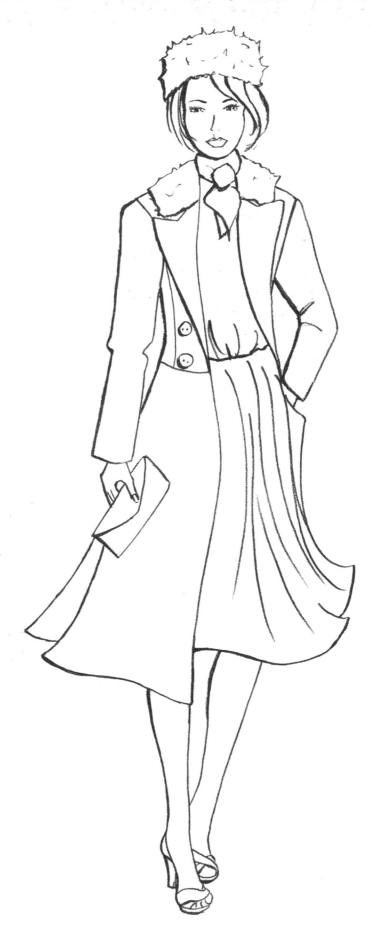

Add an Accessory

A faux fur hat to match the collar on the coat finishes off the outfit. Use a rough line for the hat to give the impression of fur.

6 Start inking in your pencil. Use thick and thin lines on the sweeping curves of the skirt and also around the coat to give the impression of weight.

Stylist's tip

To emphasize movement, kick the curves out to the side near the hem of the skirt.

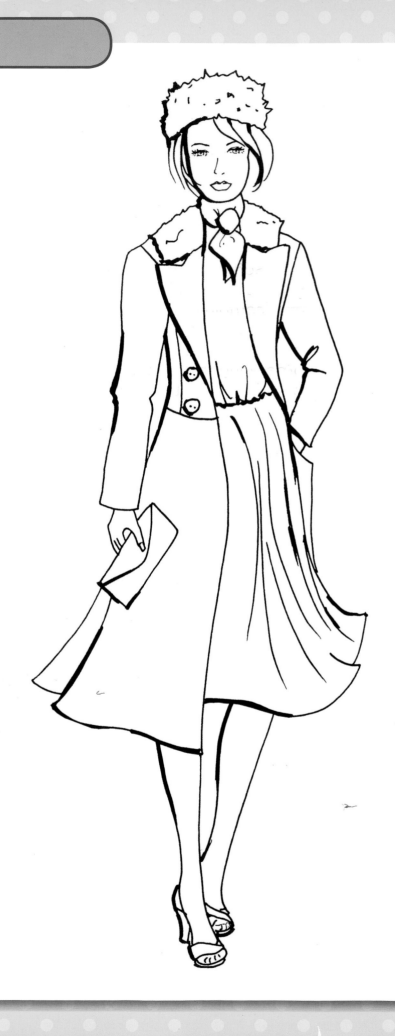

7 Soft browns and nude are used over a combination of bright red and orange for the outfit. A multicoloured print scarf incorporating the colours really helps bring the outfit together.

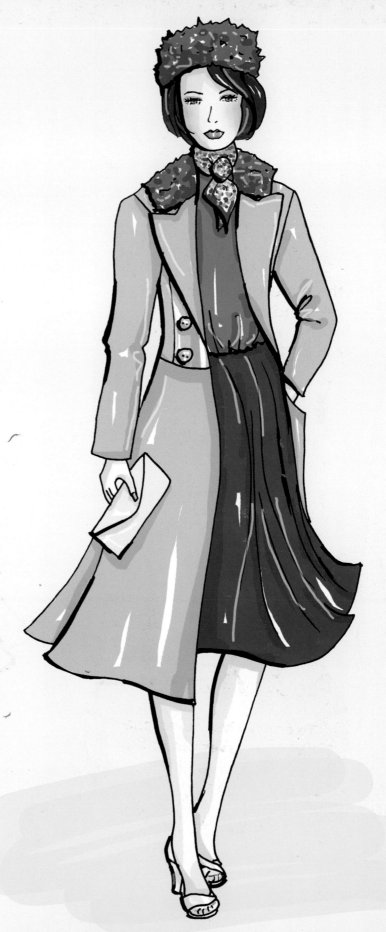

Neon Green Skirt

This bright outfit shows how a simple sleeveless white shirt can be transformed with eye-catching neon green and bright matching accessories.

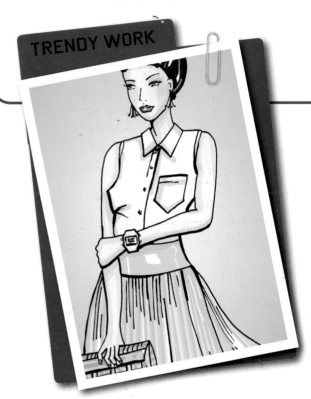

TRENDY WORK

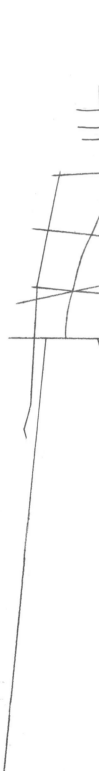

1 Draw your frame with a curve through the body to put the shoulders back and hips forward. Keep the stance with strong legs.

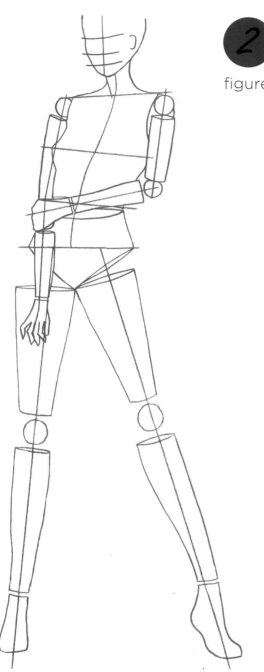

2 Create your body shape, using cylinders and balls to give the figure structure and form.

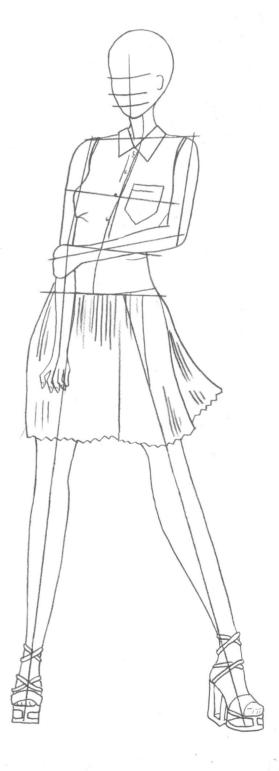

3 Start drawing in the clothing. Show the pleating on the skirt with quick lines drawn following the direction of the legs. Add a zig-zag for the hem. To make the outfit really stand out add some striking strappy heels.

4 Add the facial features and hairstyle to your sketch. By giving the model a topknot swept away from the face, you give more focus to the outfit.

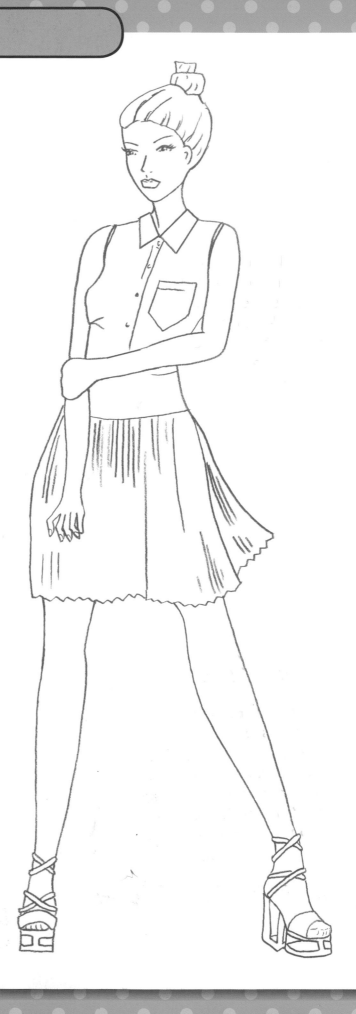

5 Make sure that when you add the pleat lines they follow the line of the skirt. Pay particular attention to the kick out at the back. Here the lines will flare out also, instead of following the line of the body.

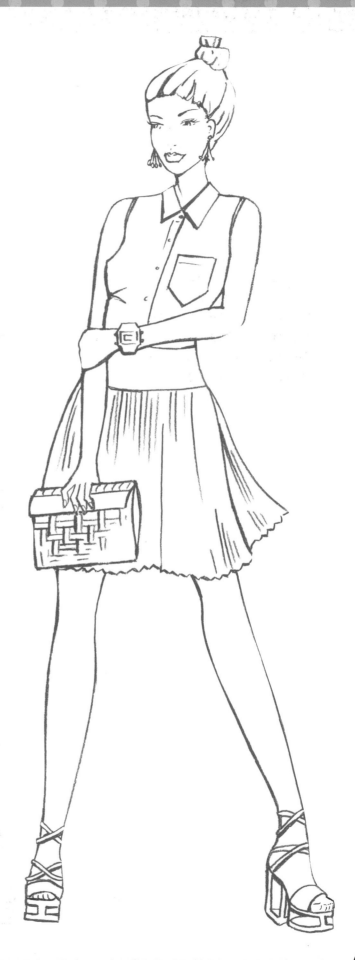

Add an Accessory

Now it's time to add the fun accessories. A chunky feature watch gives the outfit a quirky look. Drop earrings and a clutch bag mean this outfit could work on a day out or for the evening.

6 The next step is to add the ink. Work over the pencil, taking particular care with the pleats on the skirt. Also use thicker lines where the shadows will fall – for example under the collar, clutch bag flap and the skirt hem.

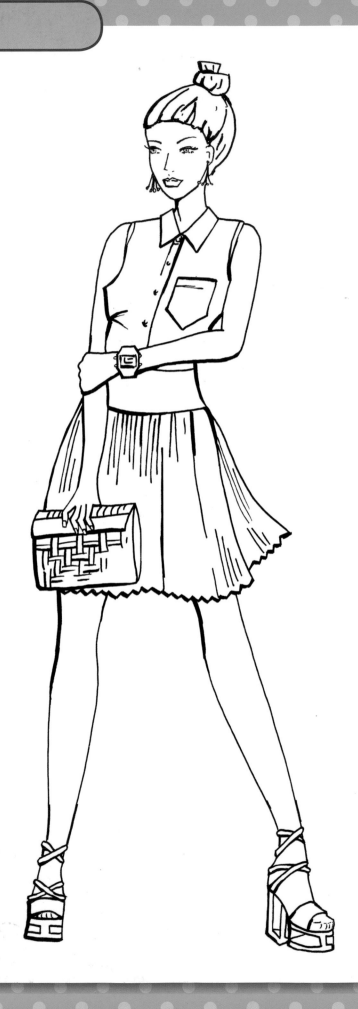

Stylist's tip

Use a dark and light green on the skirt pleats to show where the shadow and light will fall.

7 Finally, add the colour. Shade the white top with a soft grey to show the shadows. Using a bright neon green, colour the skirt and accessories. Finish off with black and neon green shoes.

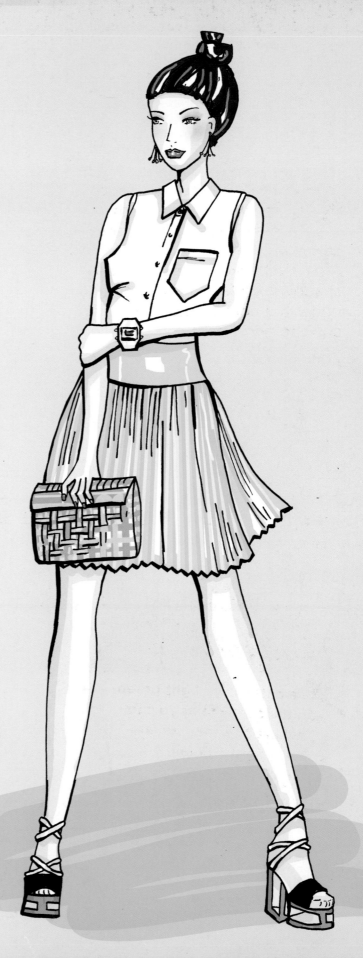

Statement Skinnies

This outfit is full of colour with dip-dye detail to the jacket over a bright orange top. Both are pulled together with a pair of multicoloured print trousers.

CASUAL DAY

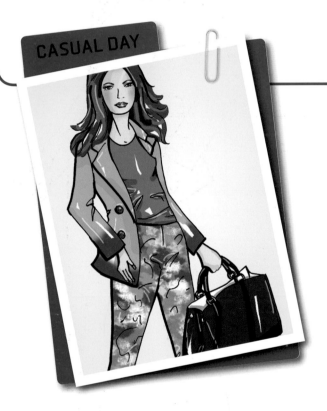

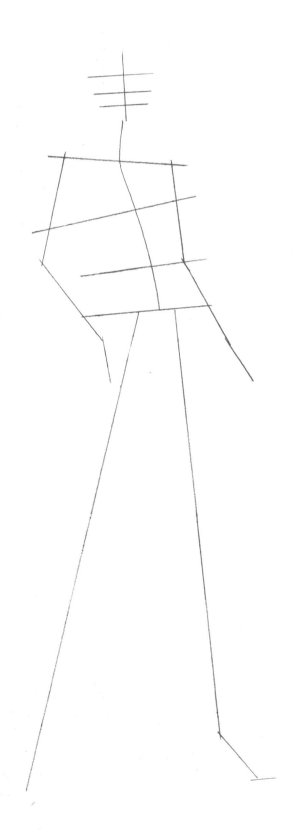

1 This is a strong pose that works well with this bold outfit. The shoulders are back and hips are pushed forward with a legs-apart stance.

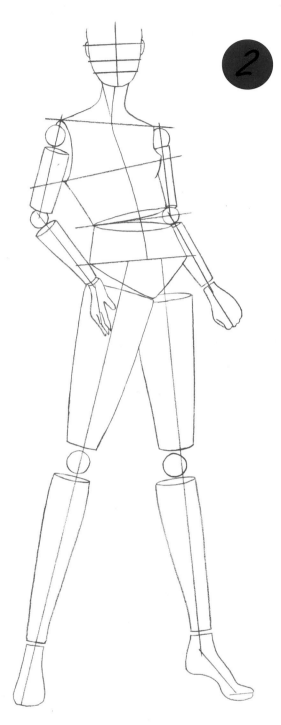

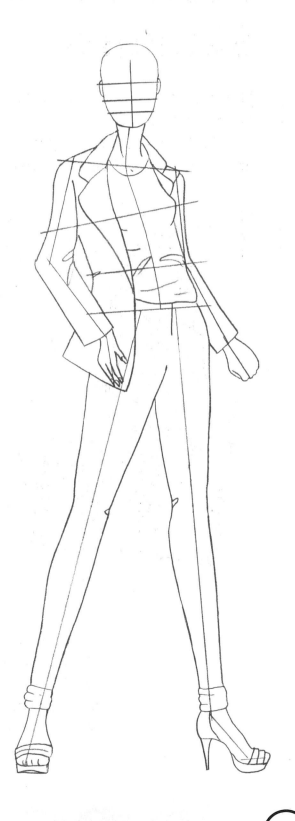

2 Add the basic shapes of cylinders and balls for the body and joints.

3 Draw the outfit onto the body. Use the curve of the body for the line of the jacket. Add detail to the top where it creases. Keep the trousers slim and straight to complement the high-heeled sandals.

4 Add the face detail and the hair. A long loose hairstyle works well with this outfit as it flows over the smart jacket collar.

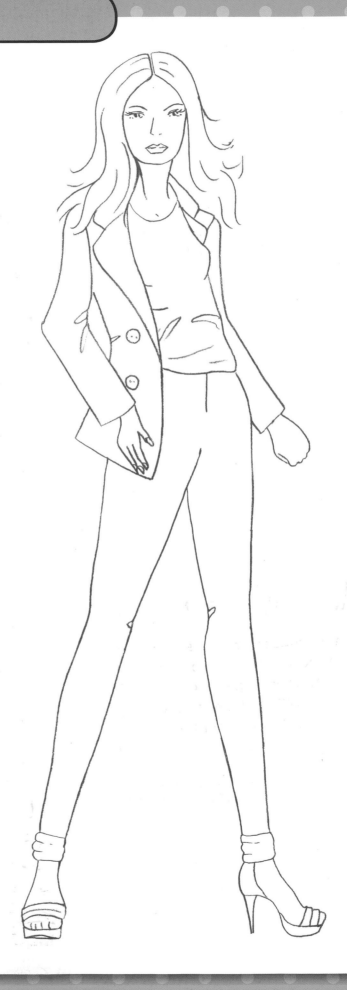

5 Now add small, curved lines to show where the print on your trousers will go.

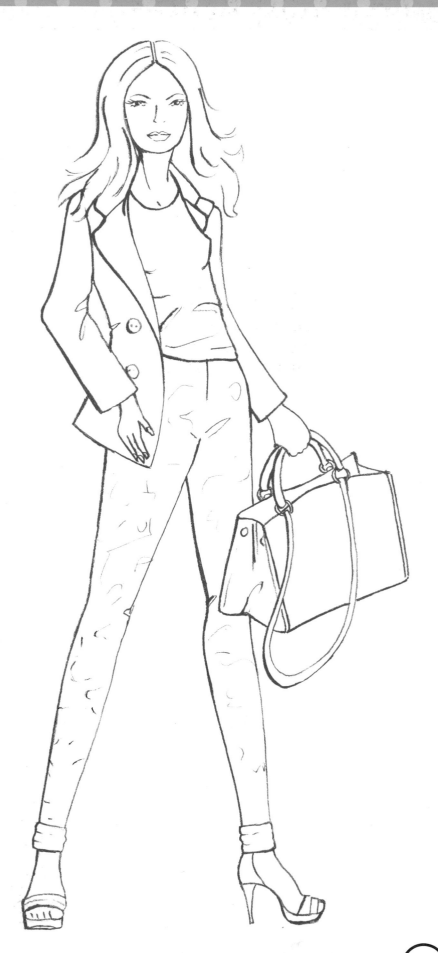

Add an Accessory

We've chosen an oversized handbag to pull this outfit together. A large block of colour will contrast nicely against the busy print on the trousers.

6 Using your finished pencil as a guide, start to work on the ink. Use a heavy line for the shadows – under the jacket collar, under the shoes, down the legs and under the buttons.

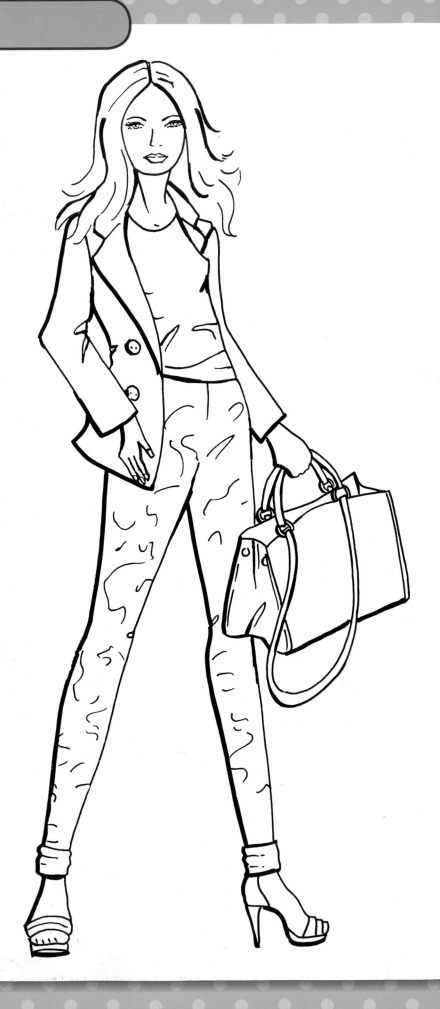

7 Working with the colour, use the orange and green from the top and the jacket for the trouser print. Add further complementary colours such as pink and yellow to make a lovely colour mix. Keep the shoes matching and the bag dark to make it really stand out.

Stylist's tip

When adding colour to the jacket, use a soft line between the two colours so one colour gently blends into the other.

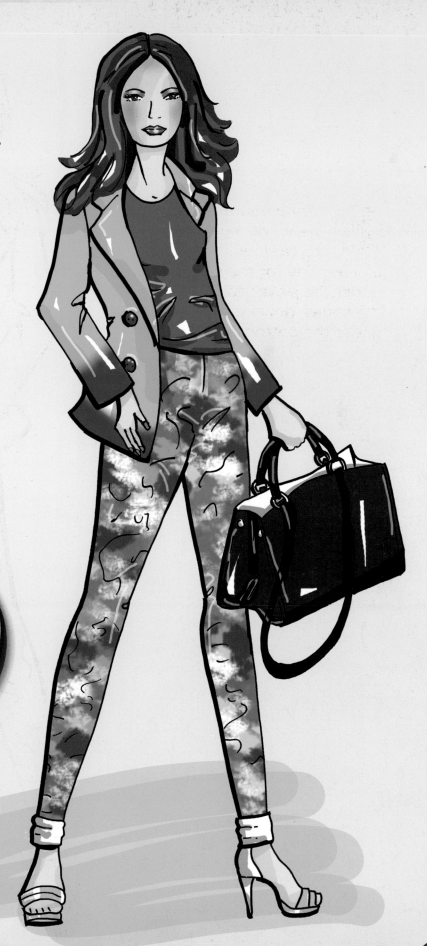

STYLE CARDS

Bright colours work well for a fresh, youthful look. You can reflect the style through some great, bright accessories. Go multicoloured or keep to one bold colour. No matter how you use your accessories, step out and have fun!

BAGS:

A bright bag can be mixed with other bright accessories or can look great on its own to enhance an outfit.

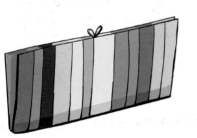

Complete the look with this multicoloured clutch.

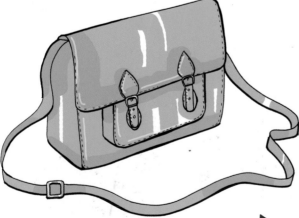

Team this bag with a simple outfit to make it really stand out.

ACCESSORIES:

Bright jewellery can be used to pull any outfit together. Adding bold necklaces or delicate earrings to an outfit can be key. Keep it light, bright and fun.

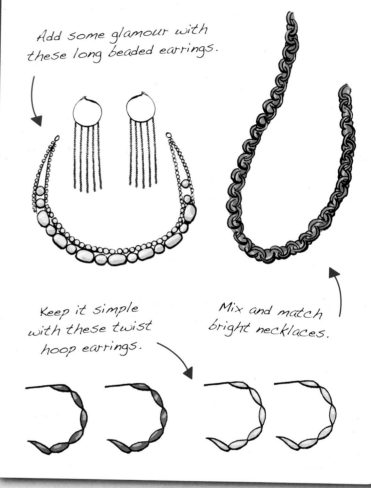

Add some glamour with these long beaded earrings.

Keep it simple with these twist hoop earrings.

Mix and match bright necklaces.

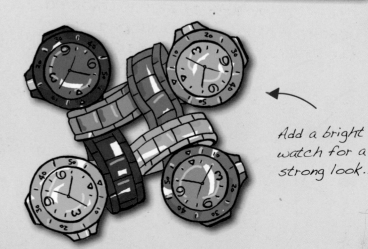

Add a bright watch for a strong look.

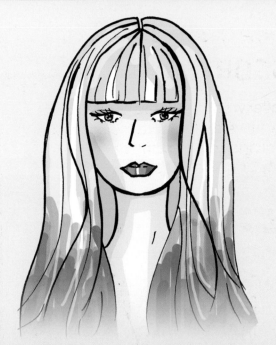

Be brave and bold with this dip-dye hairstyle.

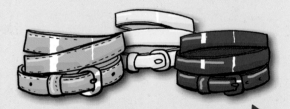

Brighten up a pair of simple black trousers with these super bright belts.

SHOES:

Keep it bright all the way to your toes with these fabulous shoes. For bright summer style use wedges, sandals or pumps.

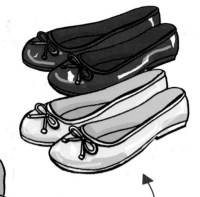

Step out in these slip-on sandals.

It's bright and shiny with these patent pumps.

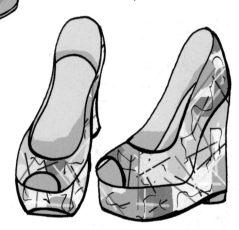

For evening or day these paint-thrown wedges make a statement.

NAILS:

For bright-style nails use multicoloured shades. Add extra nail paint patterns over the top to really make a statement.

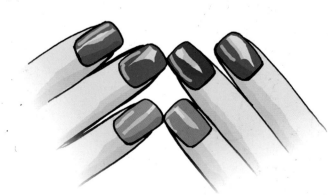

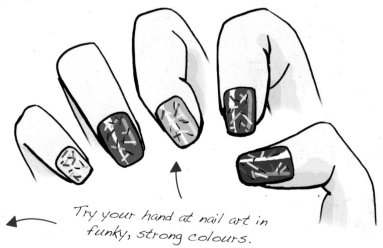

Try your hand at nail art in funky, strong colours.

VINTAGE CHIC

"Vintage" is the new buzzword in fashion. But with retro flair comes a danger. Make sure you get the styling spot-on and pair your outfit with the perfect accessories to ensure your look is glam and not granny...

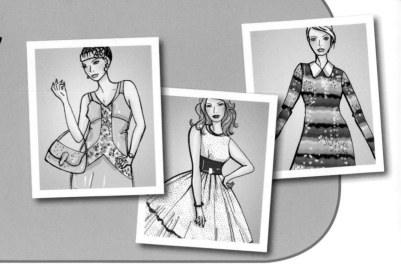

1920s Flapper Dress

VINTAGE GLAM

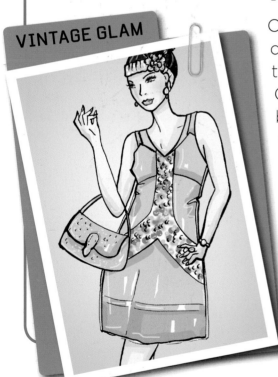

One of the most influential designers of the 1920s was the French designer, Coco Chanel. Her Flapper Dress became iconic as it portrayed women's new freedom of movement. This dress has a wonderful floaty feel and the sequin panel adds glamour. The feature sparkly headband and ostrich skin handbag completes the vintage look.

1 This outfit needs a pose to show off all the accessories. A curve through the body works well to demonstrate the hang of the dress.

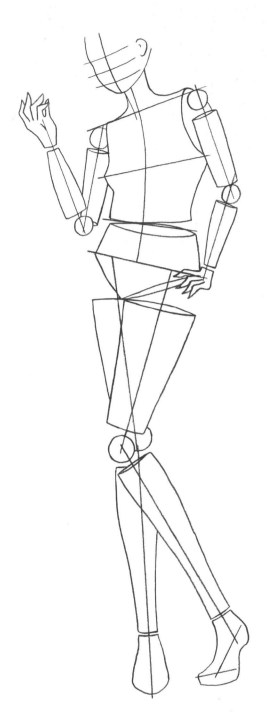

2 Work up the body structure using the basic shapes. The bend in the knee complements the model's raised right arm.

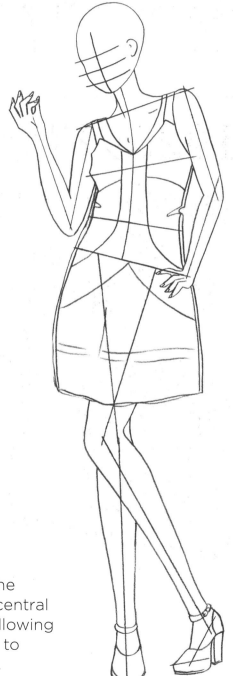

3 Add the shape of the dress. Draw in the central sequinned panel following the curved line in the body to keep it in the correct place.

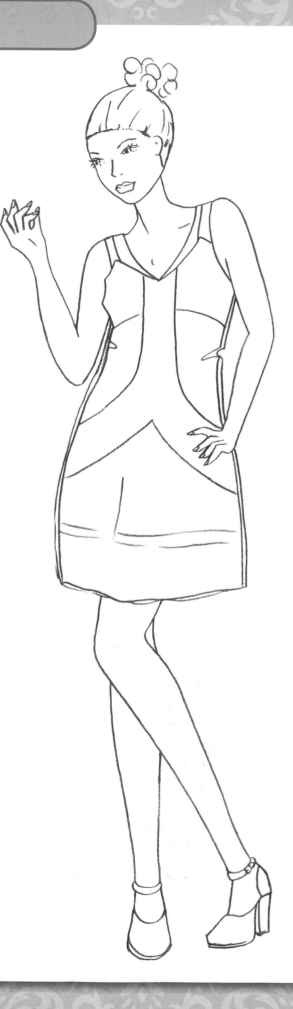

4 A classic 1920s up-do works well with this outfit, keeping the hair away from the face. Add the facial features, and remember you can use the hand as a focal point for the eyes.

5 The watch and dress ring are best shown if placed on the hand opposite the raised one. Drop earrings complement the hair, and the outfit is then topped off with a gorgeous sparkling headband with flower detail.

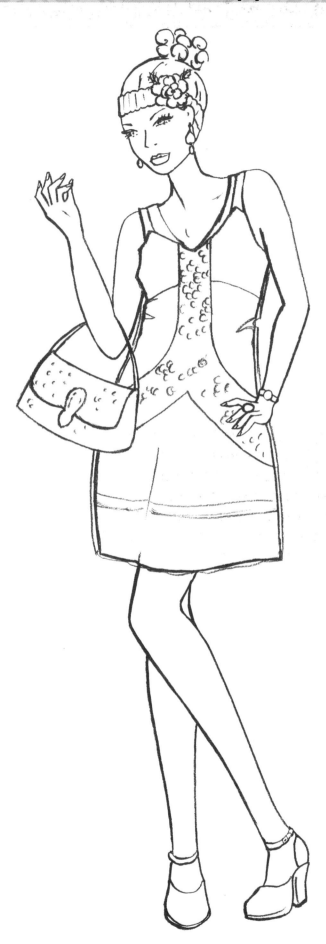

Add an Accessory

To focus attention on the sparkly panel in your dress, add a small bag in a complementary colour. Place the handbag in the elbow of the raised arm – by putting it at an angle, you give it some movement.

6 When adding the ink, use a dotting detail on the bag to show the ostrich embossing. Also show the large sequins on the panel, but only in patches, rather than all over. Take care when inking the chiffon as this line needs to be very light and can even disappear in places.

Stylist's tip

Check out vintage shops for fantastic clothing inspiration and accessories to enhance current outfits.

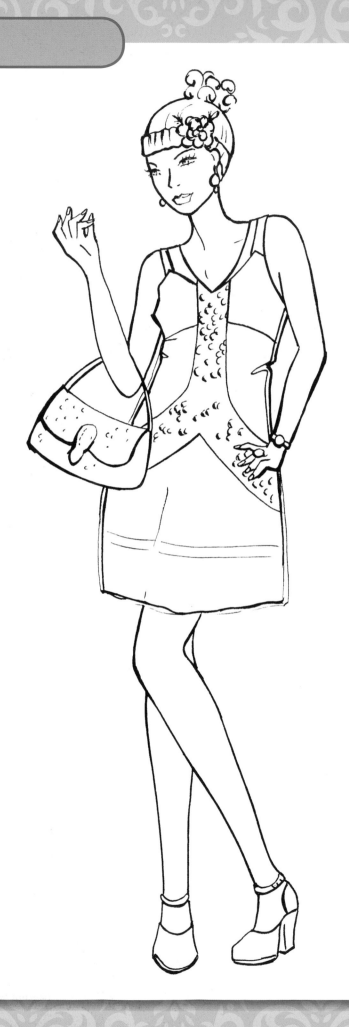

7 Ready for the colour. Pale nudes and dusty pink with just a touch of gold work well with this outfit. Keeping the colours subtle will make the most of the sparkle in the sequinned panel and headband.

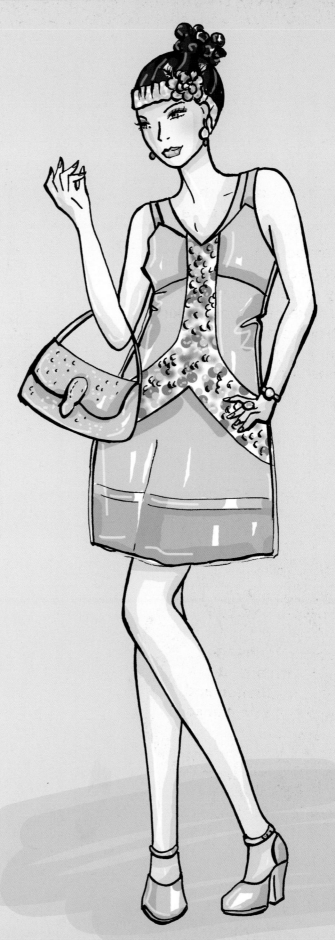

1950s Polka Dot Dress

French designer, Christian Dior became the most iconic designer of this time. He broke the mould by using much more fabric in his designs, creating dresses with swinging skirts that gave women back their curves.

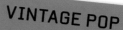

VINTAGE POP

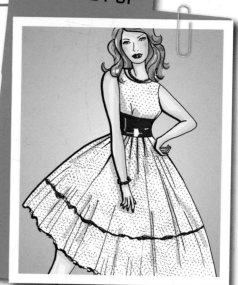

1 Create a gently curved pose for this outfit. This will show the silhouette of the dress and the fullness of the skirt.

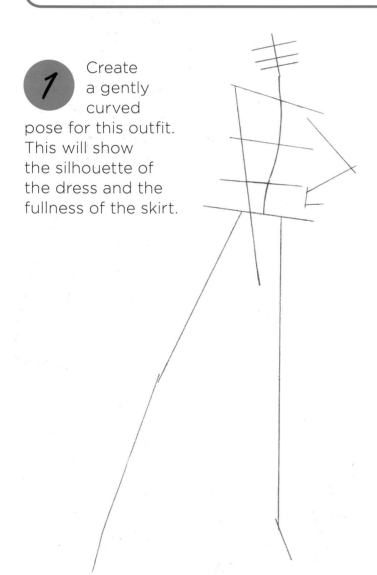

2 Add the basic shapes to fill out the body around the frame you have drawn.

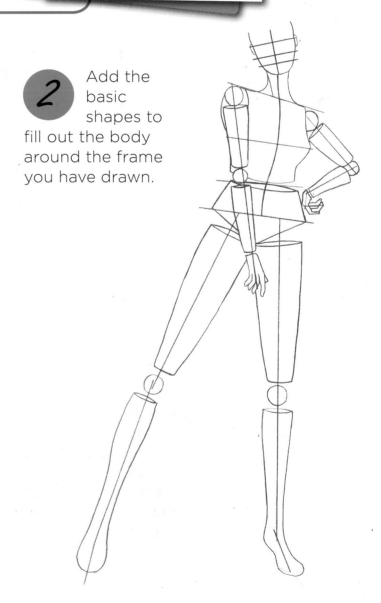

3 Put in the shape of the dress, following the lines of the body and coming out at the waist for the skirt. Add lines to show the gathering of the skirt, which indicates its fullness. Adding darts under the bust will give the dress the feel of a nipped-in waist, which was very fashionable in the 1950s. Add the basic shape of the shoe with a classic heel.

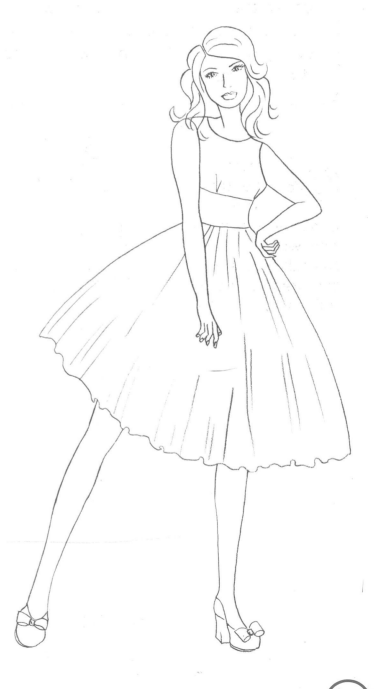

4 Giving the model a relaxed flowing hairstyle will enhance the softness of the dress and the pose that the model is in. Bow details added to the court shoes are enough to complement the simplicity of the dress.

5 Using a sharp pencil add dots to the dress. Only add the dots in patches to avoid them looking too heavy. Simple jewellery works well with this look. A beaded necklace and bracelet are enough to set off the simple dot print of the dress.

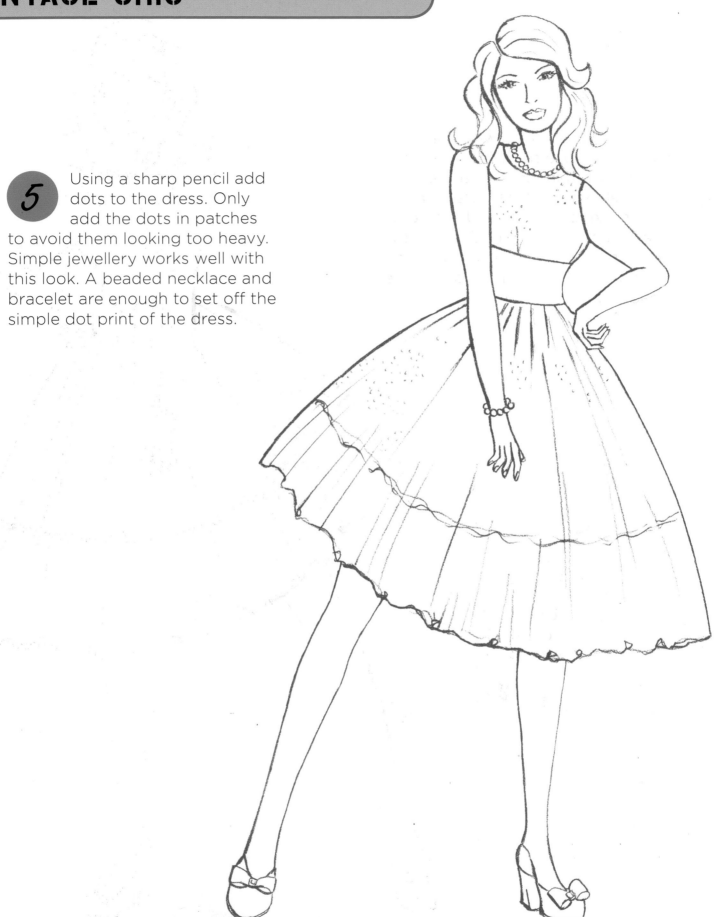

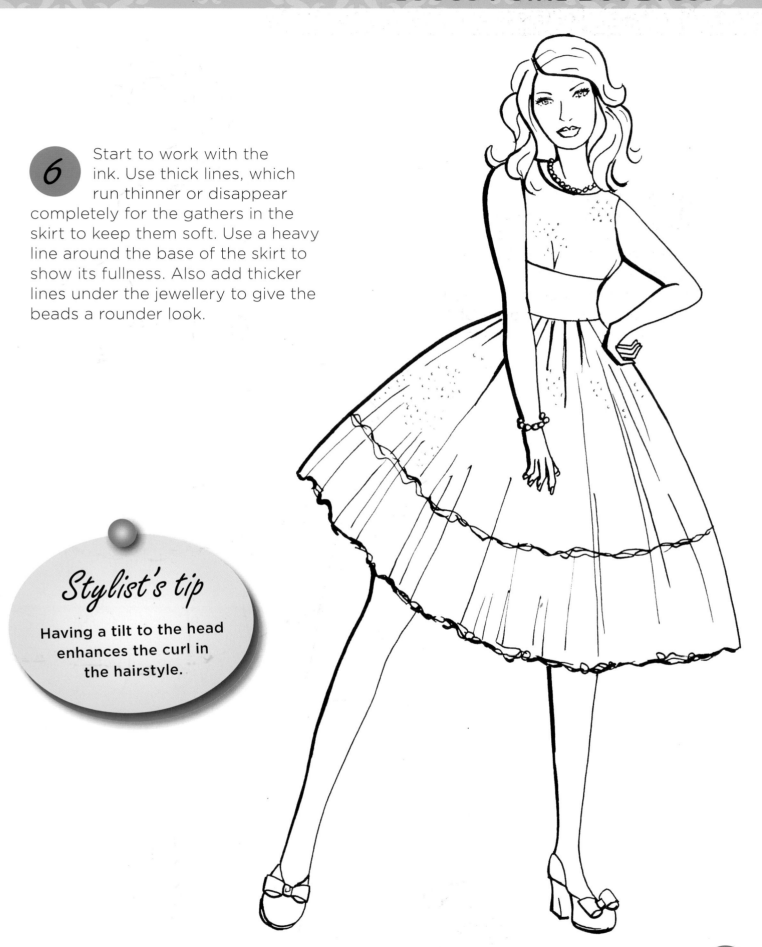

6 Start to work with the ink. Use thick lines, which run thinner or disappear completely for the gathers in the skirt to keep them soft. Use a heavy line around the base of the skirt to show its fullness. Also add thicker lines under the jewellery to give the beads a rounder look.

Stylist's tip

Having a tilt to the head enhances the curl in the hairstyle.

7 As this dress is white, we use a subtle grey to show the shadows. The red dots, skirt trim, belt, jewellery and shoes are enhanced by red lipstick and red hair. Don't forget to add sparkle to the shoes!

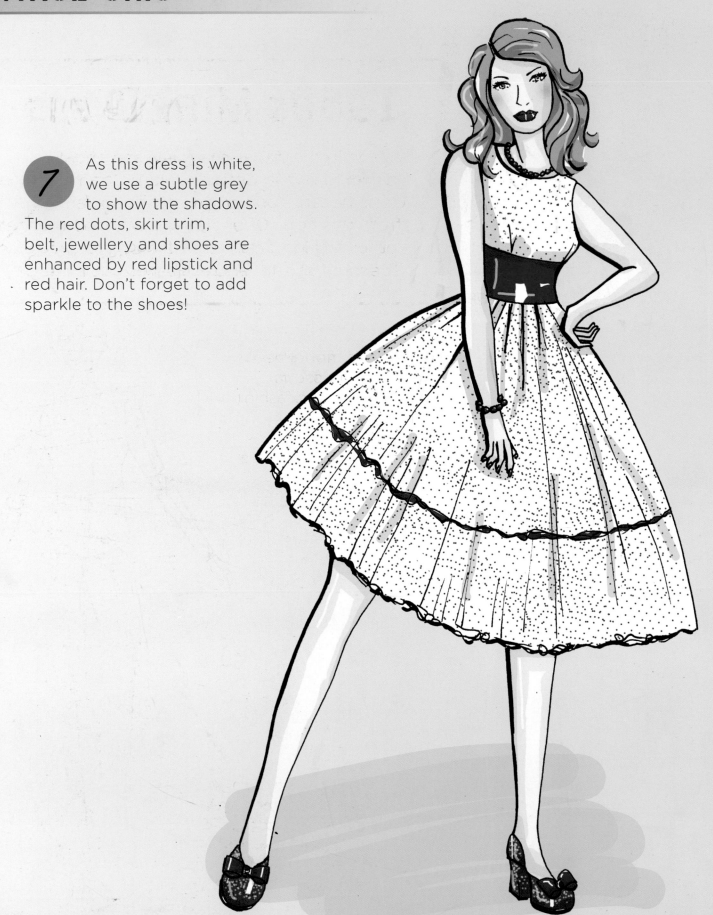

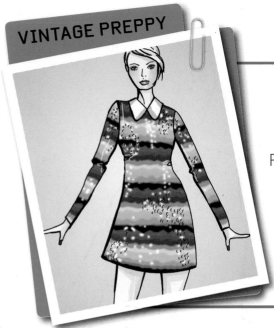

VINTAGE PREPPY

1960s Mini Dress

Fashion in the 1960s changed dramatically. Thanks to British designer, Mary Quant, the mini-dress became one of the most popular items from this time. Quant led the way and changed other fashion designers' attitudes forever. Skirts became shorter and eyelashes got longer!

1 This model needs a fun pose to reflect the fashion of the 1960s. Create your frame using clear lines showing the figure's proportions.

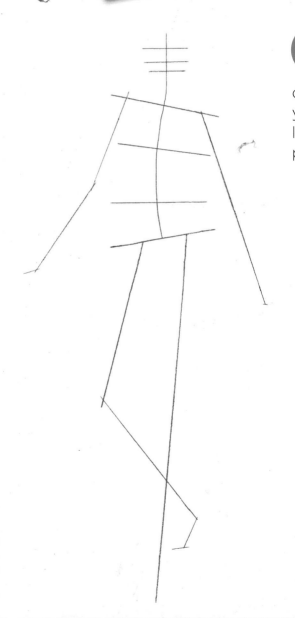

2 Build on your frame using basic shapes. The cylinder and ball shapes create the structure of the body.

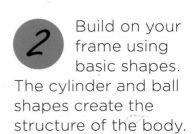

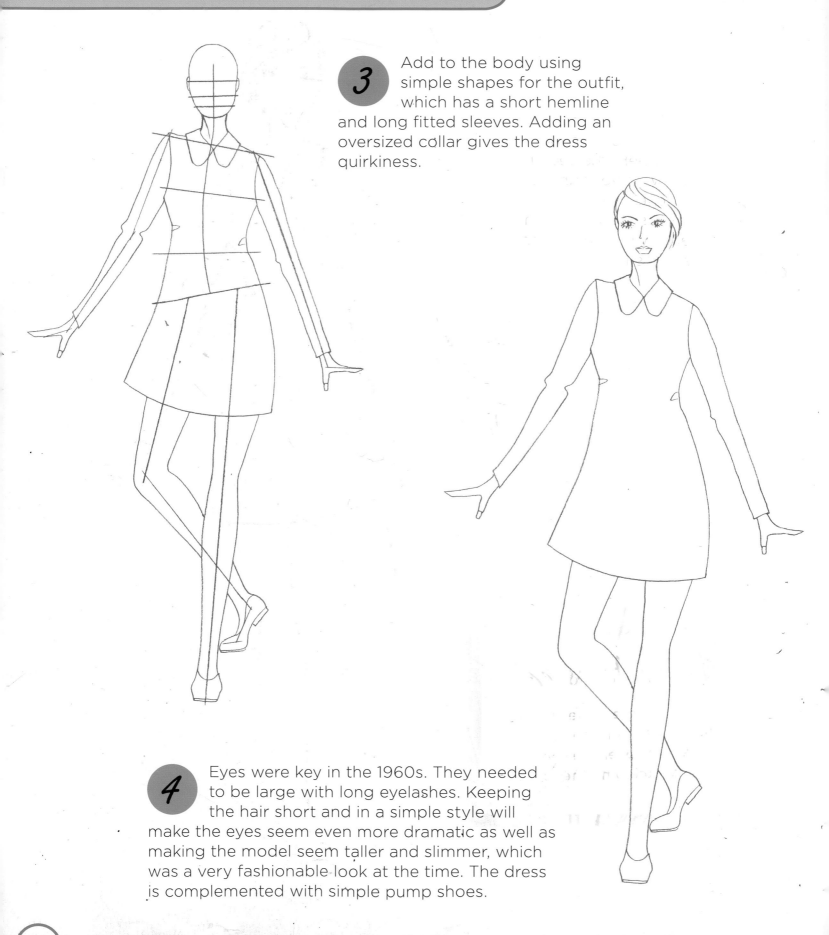

3 Add to the body using simple shapes for the outfit, which has a short hemline and long fitted sleeves. Adding an oversized collar gives the dress quirkiness.

4 Eyes were key in the 1960s. They needed to be large with long eyelashes. Keeping the hair short and in a simple style will make the eyes seem even more dramatic as well as making the model seem taller and slimmer, which was a very fashionable look at the time. The dress is complemented with simple pump shoes.

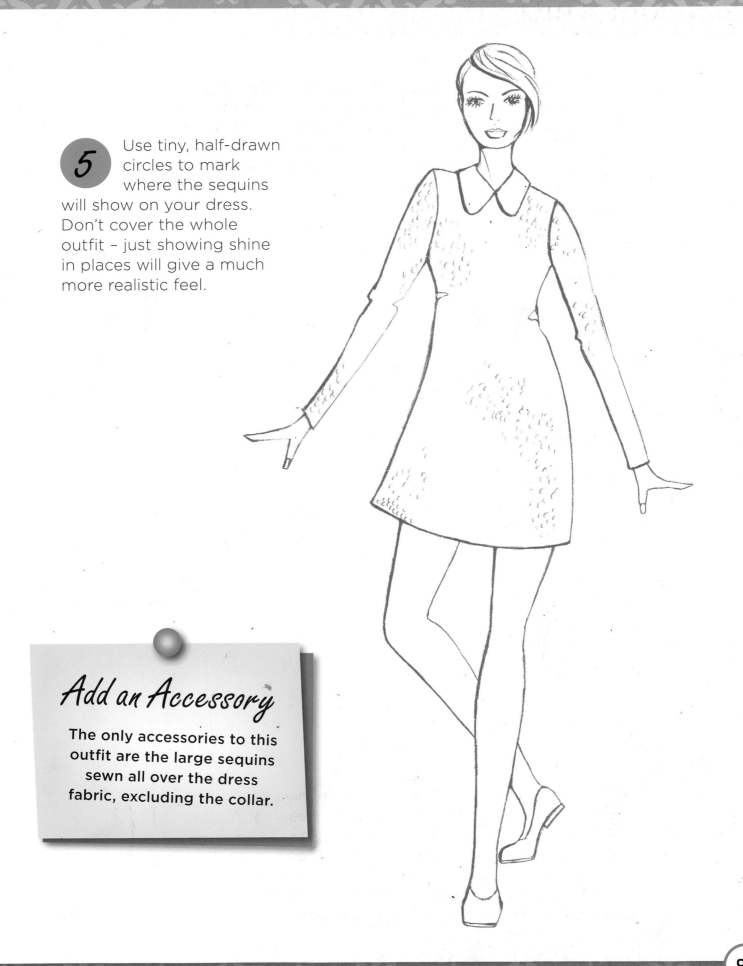

5 Use tiny, half-drawn circles to mark where the sequins will show on your dress. Don't cover the whole outfit – just showing shine in places will give a much more realistic feel.

Add an Accessory

The only accessories to this outfit are the large sequins sewn all over the dress fabric, excluding the collar.

6 Time for the ink. Working over the pencil, pay attention to where there will be shadows – under the collar and also under the fringe on the face.

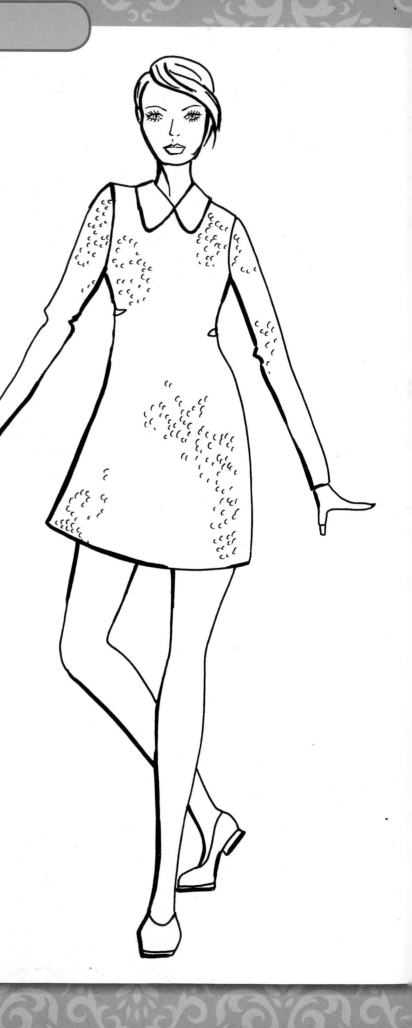

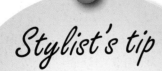

Stylist's tip

Use soft lines for your coloured stripes to give the impression of the colours running into each other, like a rainbow.

7 The final step is for colour. Bold rainbow colours are used all the way down the dress and the sleeves. Adding large dots of white to the dress gives the impression of light reflecting off the sequins.

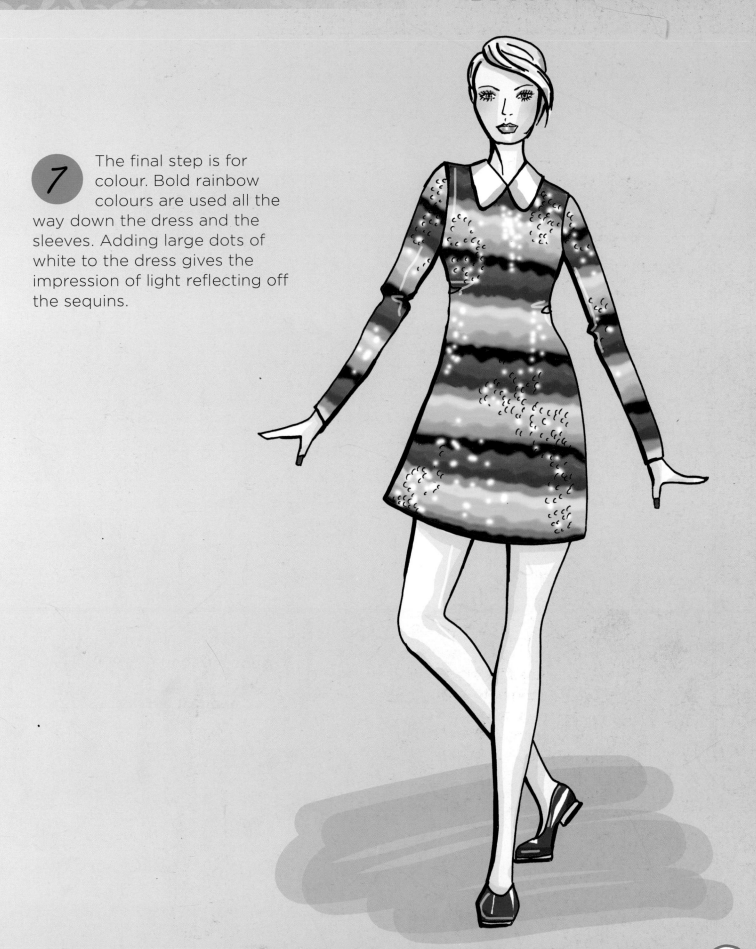

STYLE CARDS

Vintage-style accessories are everywhere. Whether you are hitting the high street or raiding your mum's wardrobe it is totally on trend. Accessorising with vintage bags and shoes can really work an outfit. Go back in time and get inspired!

1920s:

Pearls, beads and hair accessories have the wow factor from this decade.

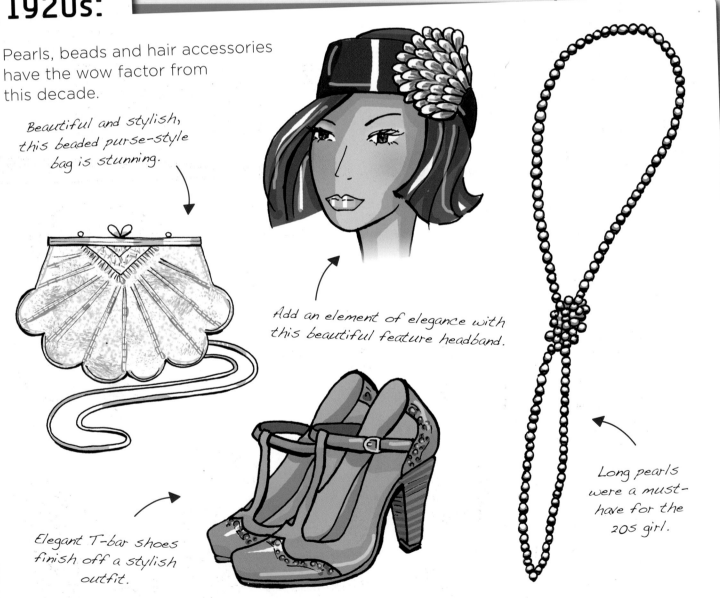

Beautiful and stylish, this beaded purse-style bag is stunning.

Add an element of elegance with this beautiful feature headband.

Elegant T-bar shoes finish off a stylish outfit.

Long pearls were a must-have for the 20s girl.

1950s:

The 1950s accessory style is feminine and stylish, from pretty heeled shoes to girly glasses.

This bowling-style bag is a great addition to any outfit.

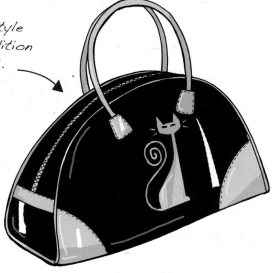

Pretty polka dots are a must for the 1950s style.

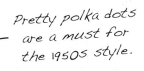

Make a statement with these 50s style glasses... not for hiding behind!

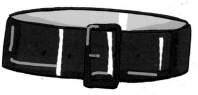

Add a thick belt for a perfect nipped-in waist and strong silhouette.

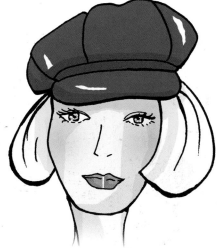

1960s:

Be bright, be bold and stand out. The 1960s accessories are fun and fabulous!

Top off your outfit with a stylish cap.

For the ultimate 60s hairstyle it has to be a beehive.

Keep things colourful with bright and funky dress rings.

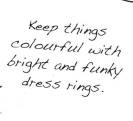

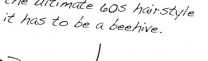

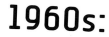

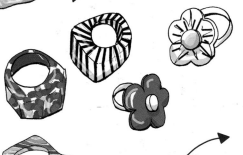

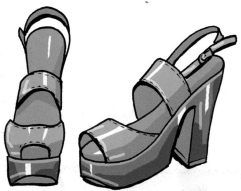

These bold wedges make a statement!

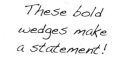

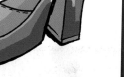

SPORTS LUXE

Score some fashion points this season with sports-inspired clothing. Items straight out of the sports hall are paired with glamorous accessories for outfits that are sure to win gold!

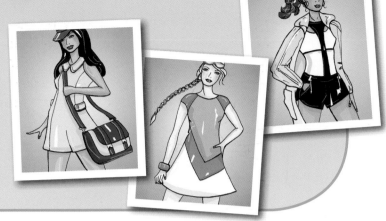

Nautical Playsuit

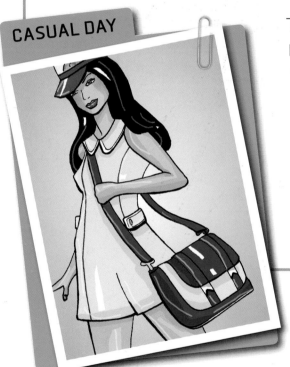

This fun sporty playsuit is a great addition to any wardrobe. Accessorized with an oversized satchel bag, wedges and a sporty visor, it is ideal for fun in the sun.

1 For a fun outfit you need a fun model. Start with straight lines for your frame, adding a strong curve to the body and straight legs.

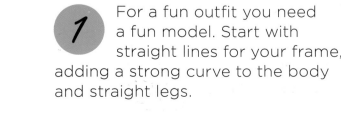

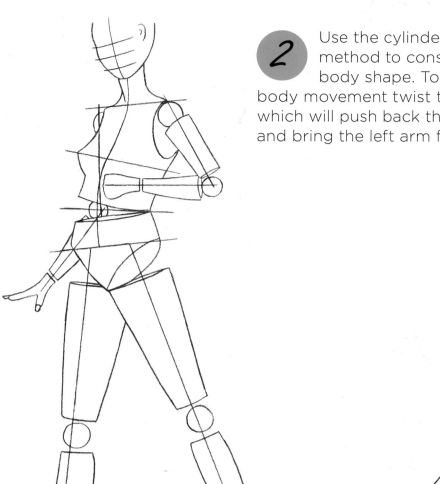

2 Use the cylinder and ball method to construct the body shape. To give the body movement twist the torso, which will push back the right arm and bring the left arm forward.

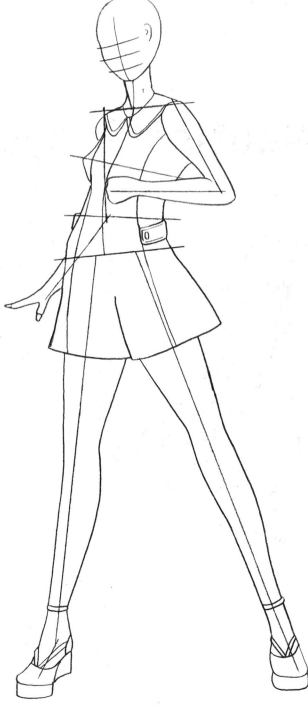

3 Draw the playsuit shape over the body with the collar and side tab details. The shorts need to follow the direction of the legs. Now add the wedged sandals with strap detail.

4 Give this model a long soft hairstyle with a side parting, which sits well over the shoulders. Keep the collar free so it is highlighted as a feature. Also add the facial details.

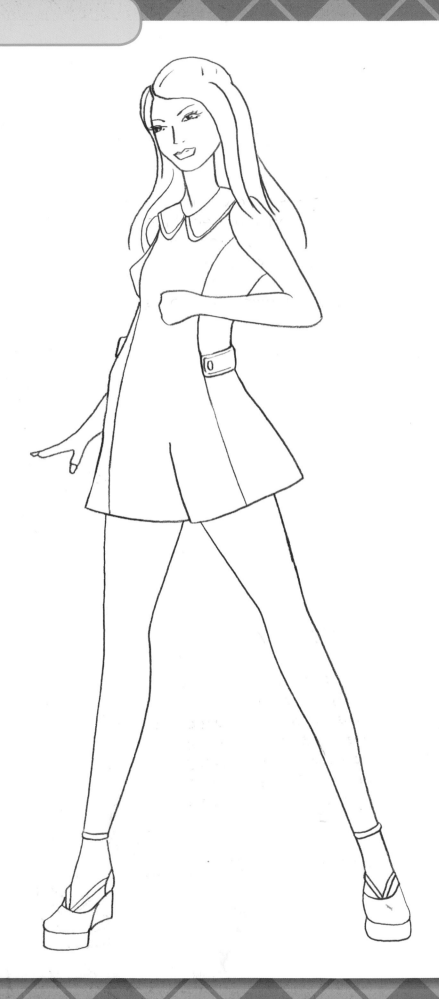

5 Before you ink, focus on your pencil lines. Make sure your shorts are well defined, otherwise your playsuit could end up looking like a dress!

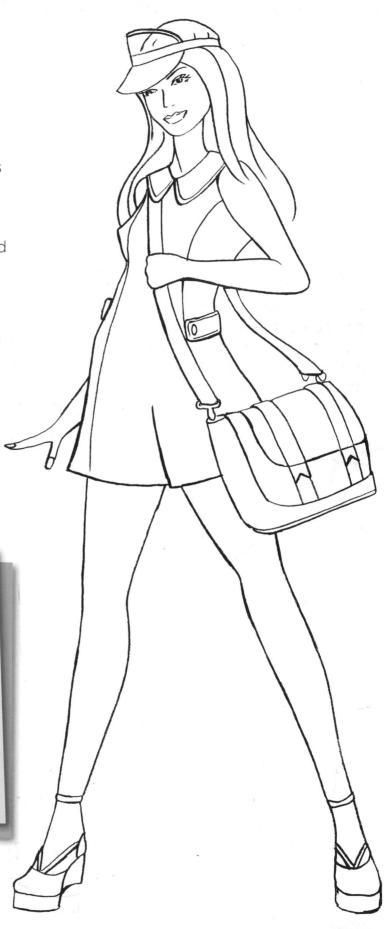

Add an Accessory

To accessorize this outfit, a sporty oversized bag is worn across the body. Draw the bag strap underneath the collar, to keep the collar detail a feature of the playsuit. Top off the outfit with a fun matching visor.

6 Now ink your drawing. Fluid lines create a structured look to the outfit but still keep the look soft. Use heavier lines around the collar detail, side tabs and sun visor to make them really stand out.

Stylist's tip

Taking a little extra care over the fine details like seam lines, buttons and straps can make all the difference to your drawing.

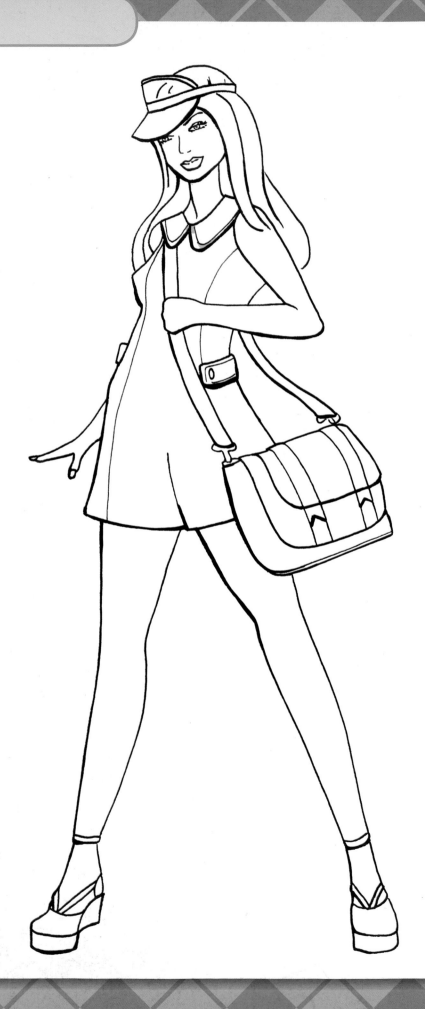

7 Light and dark shades of blue, with red highlights and the odd touch of white, give this outfit a fun nautical feel. Complement with dark hair and tanned skin to give it a really summery look.

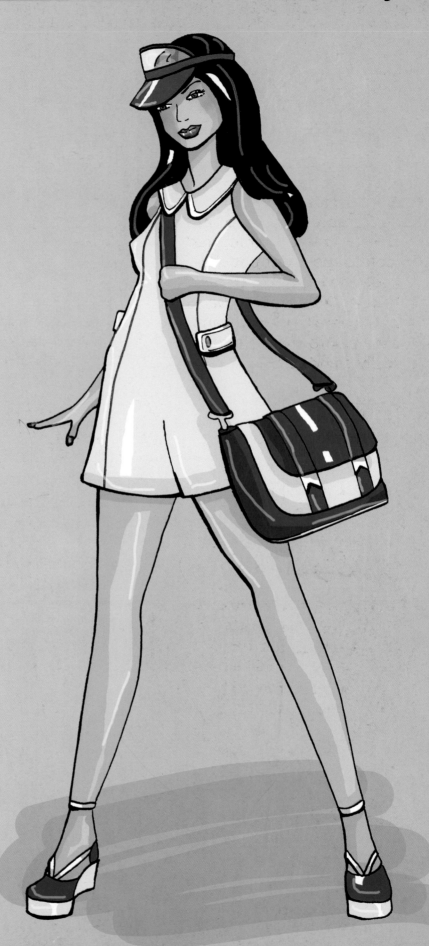

SPORTY DAY

Tennis Dress

This little sporty dress is perfect for summer days out and has a definite chic style. Adding a pair of ankle socks with a ruffled trim gives the outfit a girly feel.

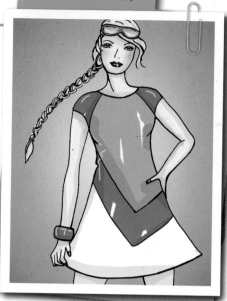

1 For this pose keep the frame lines straight, giving a gentle tilt to the head and a pointed toe.

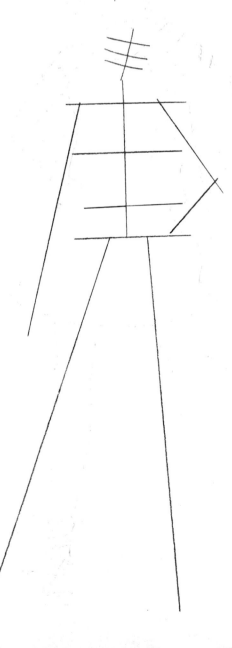

2 Build out the body shape with the cylinder and ball shapes.

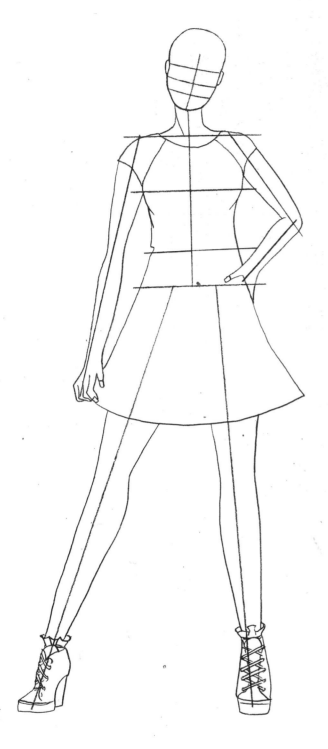

3 Now for the outfit. Draw in the dress over your body shape, giving a small flare to the skirt. Also at this step add a pair of heeled trainers with laces and some sweet, ruffle ankle socks.

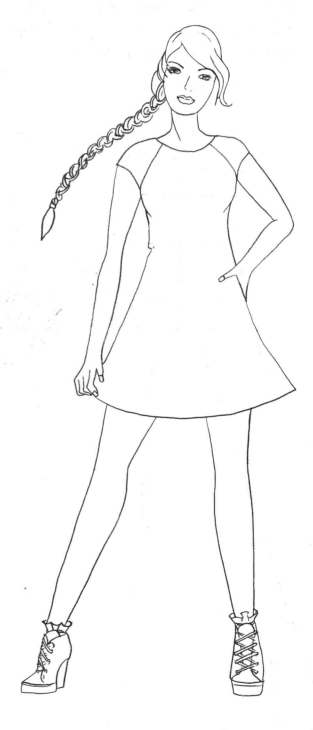

4 Sketch in the facial features and hairstyle. A sporty long plait looks great with this outfit. Swinging the plait away from the body gives the model movement. Keep the hair soft around the face to add to the girly feel.

5 Simple chic accessories need to be used with this outfit, try a lovely chunky bracelet with a pair of sunglasses placed on the model's head. Add the panel detail to the front of the dress.

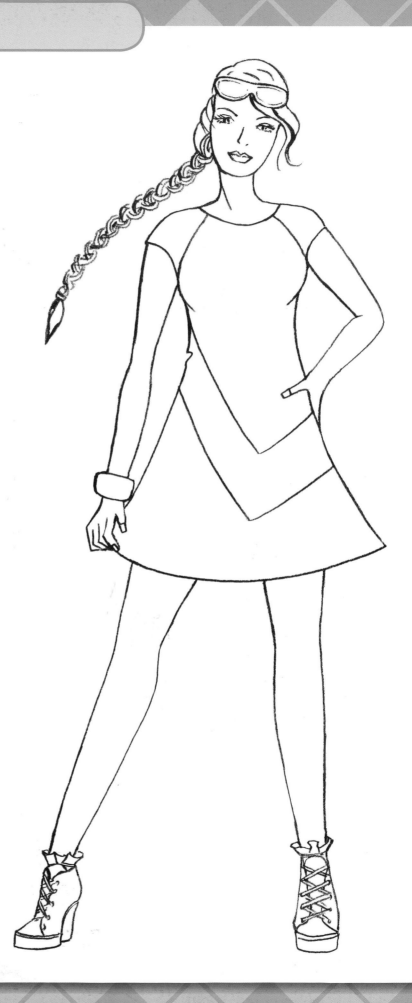

6 Time to ink your pencil. Use a heavy line around the skirt base and the underside of the bracelet and sunglasses. Take care when drawing the plait, keeping the lines fine and neat to give definition.

Stylist's tip

Help to lift your picture by adding darker lines to the underside of the shoe laces and around the sock ruffles.

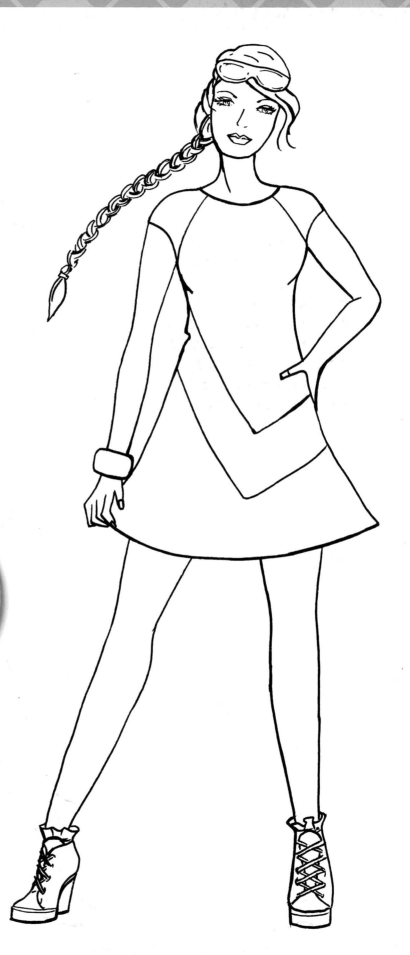

7 Working up the colour, a combination of fawn, orange and cream is used for the dress. The outfit is tied together with matching orange accessories. A bright colour is also used for the lipstick and nails.

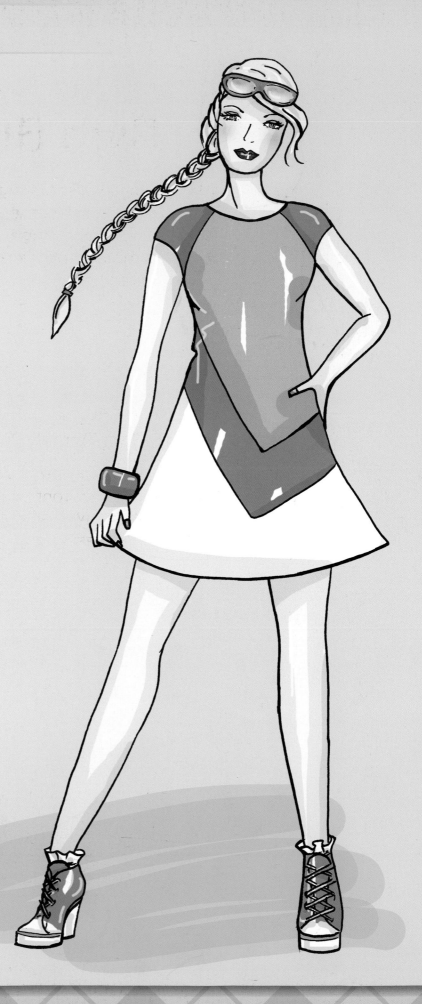

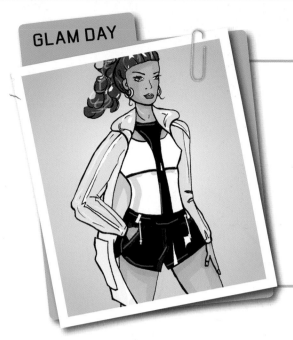

GLAM DAY

Gym Glam

Not for a shrinking violet, this outfit really makes a statement. The colours are strong and bright and it looks great with simple hoop earrings and, of course, killer heels.

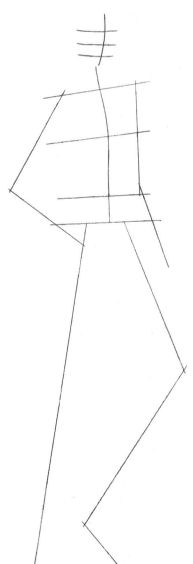

1 Your first step is to create your simple frame using straight lines. For this pose, give the front knee a bend to give the model a casual feel.

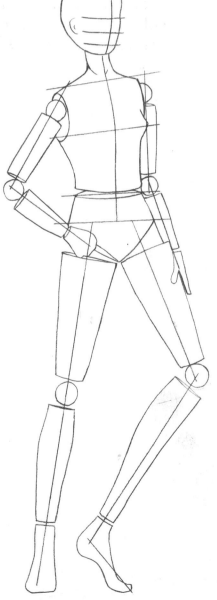

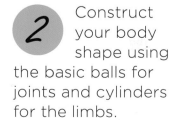

2 Construct your body shape using the basic balls for joints and cylinders for the limbs.

SPORTS LUXE

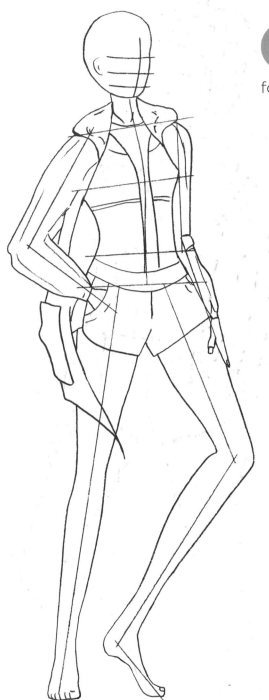

3 For this step, add the shape of the outfit over the body. Take care when adding the central panel to the outfit making sure you follow the body shape down to the hips.

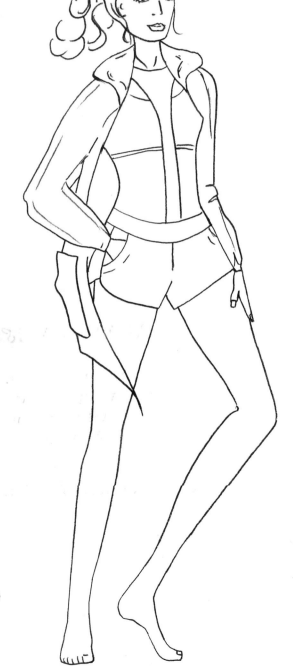

4 Add the facial detail and hairstyle at this step. For this model a high pony tail works well to give height and also lift the hair away from the neck and shoulders, keeping the hood and neck detail clear.

5 An ankle strap helps to draw attention to the model's long legs – made longer by the shortness of the outfit.

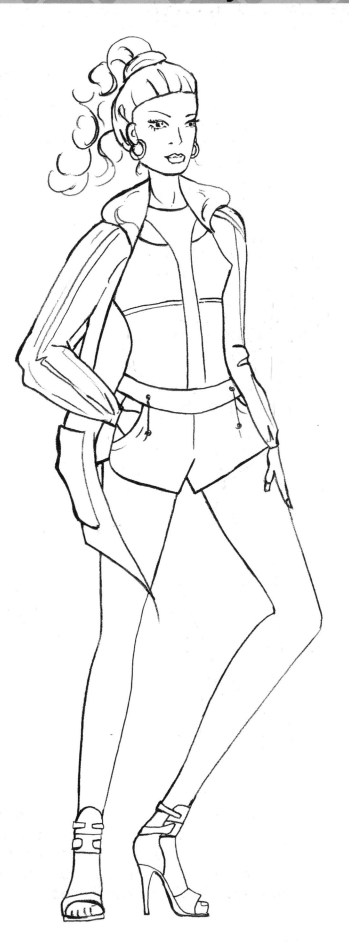

Add an Accessory

To complement the shoes, hoop earrings are added to this outfit for a touch of glamour.

6 Time to ink your finished drawing. Use fine lines for the details, such as the hanging cords on the shorts, and the seam details across the front and down the sleeves. Heavier lines can be used in the creases and under the hood.

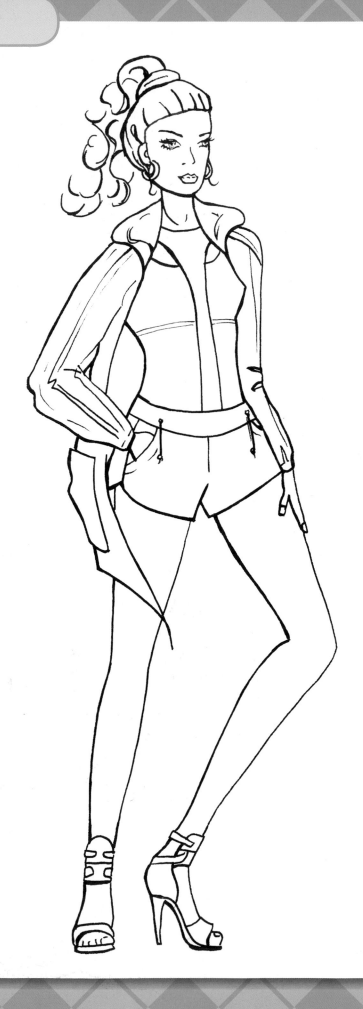

7 Light lime green teamed with black and white is used for this outfit. These colours really stand out against tanned skin and keep the look fresh. The model has strong make up to show that this outfit isn't just for the gym.

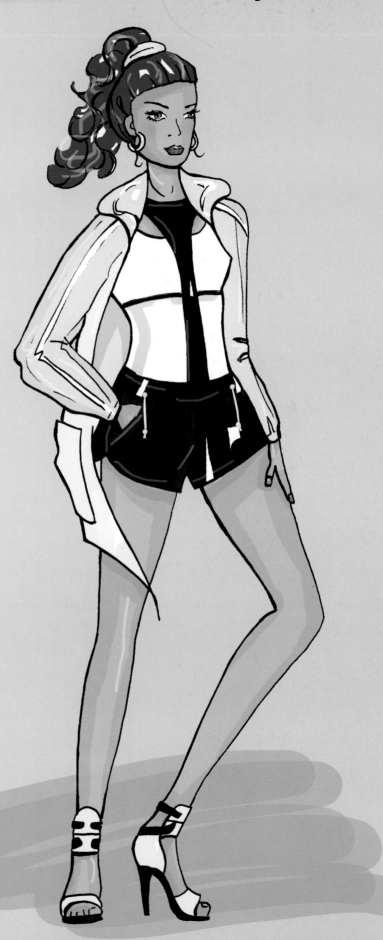

Stylist's tip

By adding a flesh colour to the coat sleeves you can show where the arms would be, which will give the impression of how sheer the jacket fabric is.

STYLE CARDS

Get the sporty look with great accessories, whether you are working out or just working the look. Here are a few items that can really give you the sporty style from the top of your head to the tips of your toes.

HAIR:

Keep the hair up and away from the face with neat hairstyles. Buns and side rolls are great to hold your hair up – and keep it there!

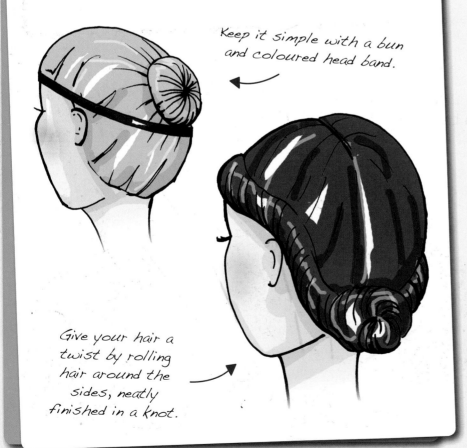

Keep it simple with a bun and coloured head band.

Give your hair a twist by rolling hair around the sides, neatly finished in a knot.

Get the sporty style with this visor – a great addition to a playsuit or short sports dress.

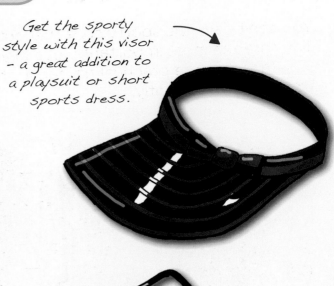

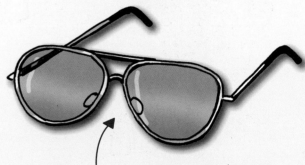

For summer-style aviator shades are the perfect addition.

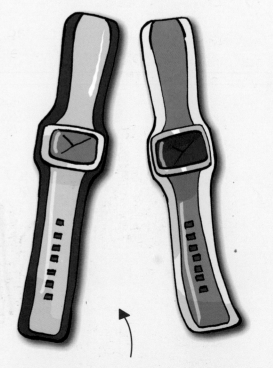

Simple and bright watches add zing to your outfit.

SHOES:

You can't have the sporty style without the perfect shoes. They are the most important piece in your outfit. Whether they are practical trainers or hot-looking heels wear them confidently.

Work the look in these killer heels.

Keep it cool with wedge trainers.

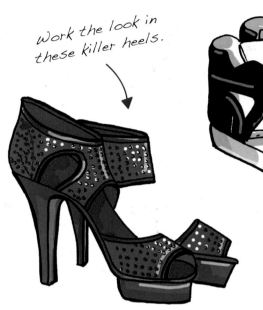
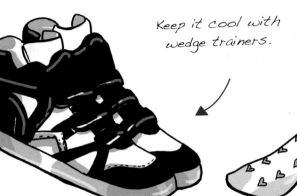
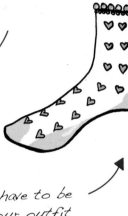
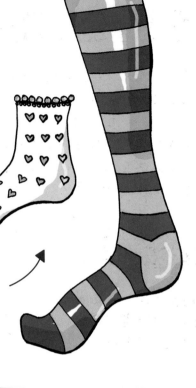

Sport socks don't have to be dull. Brighten up your outfit with bold stripes or fun heart ankle socks.

BAGS:

Whether you need a sports bag for all your kit or a small clutch for just a few coins and your keys, a bag is essential to go with your sporty outfit.

Choose a soft leather drawstring bag for a casual sports look.

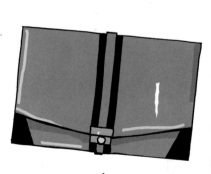
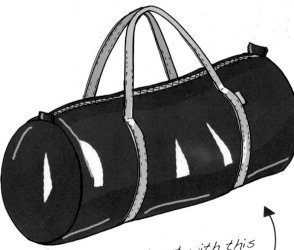
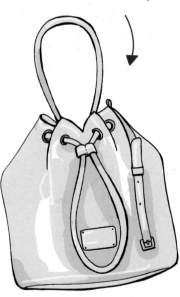

Add a touch of chic to your outfit with this racing-stripe clutch.

Stand out with this pink barrel bag.

DESIGN ICONS

A catwalk collection is only as good as its designer. Here we look at three design icons who have shaped the look of the fashion industry with their bold statements and timeless designs.

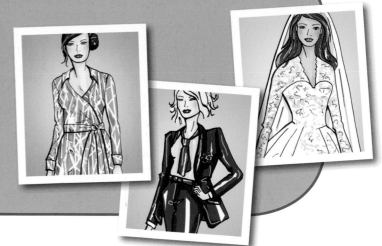

Diane von Furstenberg

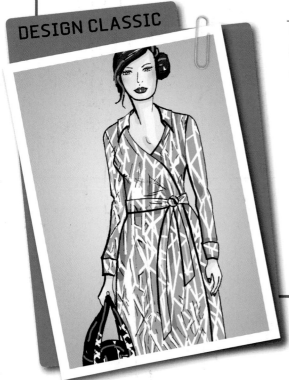

DESIGN CLASSIC

This iconic wrap-around dress was created in 1972 for professional women that needed stylish, easy to wear work attire. An exciting print works well with the simple, figure flattering shape.

1 Begin by drawing your body frame. This is a very simple pose, so keep the lines straight with a small curve for the body.

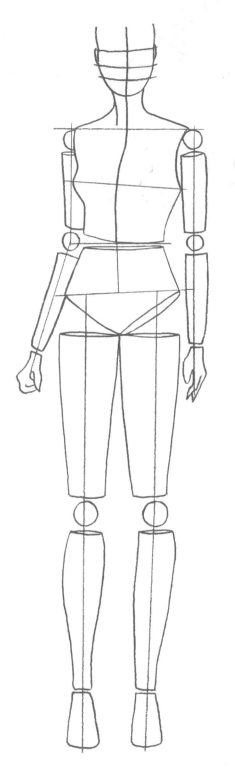

2 Build up the body, using your cylinder and ball shapes.

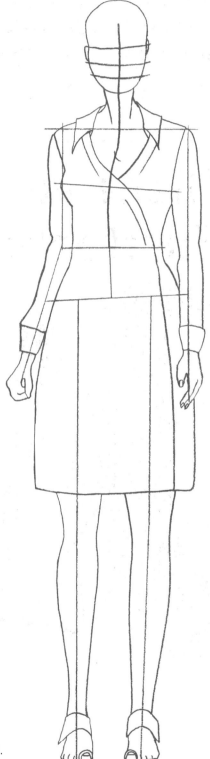

3 Over the top of the body shape, following your frame, place your dress outline. Add a simple pair of sandals to complement the dress.

4 Time for the hairstyle and facial features. A fashionable low side-bun works well with this dress – by keeping the hair away from the neck, you can really show the shape of the neckline and collar. Add a knotted belt and show the creases in the dress where the belt will pull in the fabric.

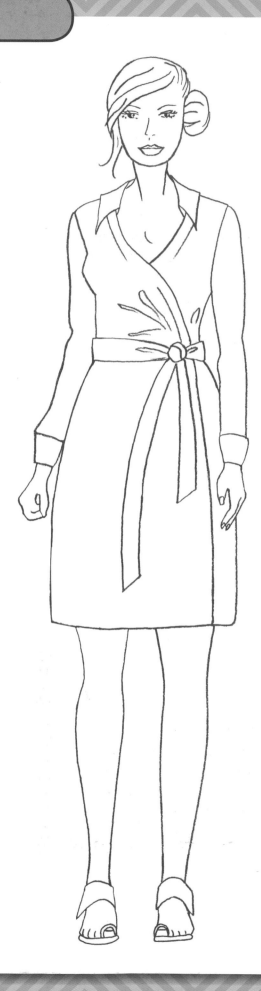

5 Now is the time to add the impression of the dress. Straight lines scattered all over the dress will work best. Don't forget to add a different print to your bag.

Add an Accessory

With this outfit we have chosen just one accessory – a big bold statement handbag with a contrasting print.

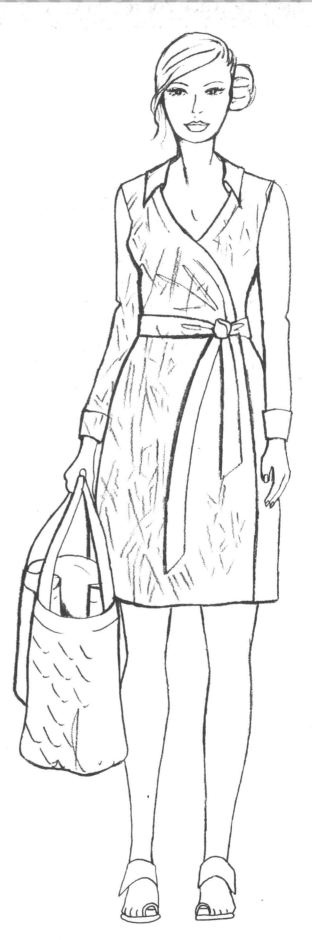

6 Begin inking your pencil when you are happy with your finished drawing. Use thicker lines around the dress, under the belt and around the bag and sandals. Also use a thicker line on the inside of the bun to make the hairstyle work as a feature. Keep the lines in the print light and thin.

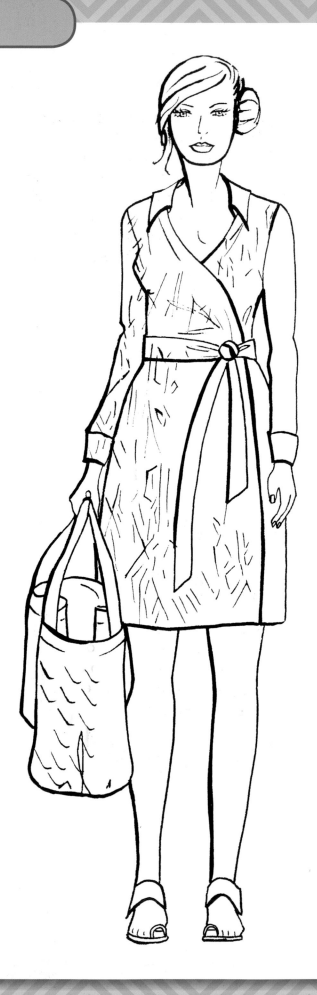

7 Time to add the colour to your ink. A sky blue works well with an exciting white print. Use a darker blue for the sandals, as these will be accentuated by the darker shadows in the dress. Finish off by colouring the bag black with a white print.

Stylist's tip

When creating a printed fabric, use a darker shade of colour in the shadow so you do not lose the body shape in a busy print.

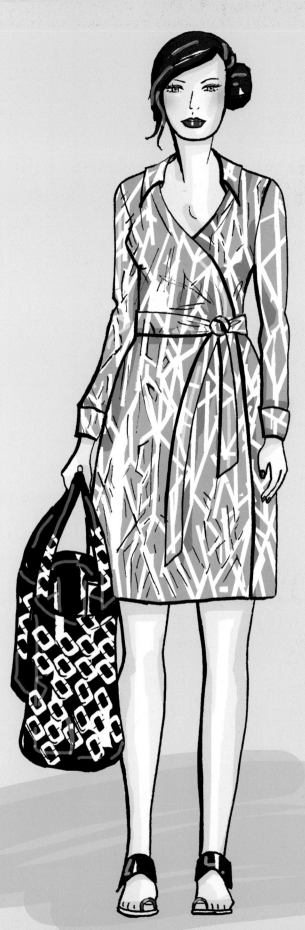

Yves Saint Laurent

YSL created the famous 'Le Smoking' tuxedo suit for women in 1966. He pioneered the androgynous style for women. This beautifully tailored tuxedo is given a feminine touch with fuchsia pink accessories.

TAILORING

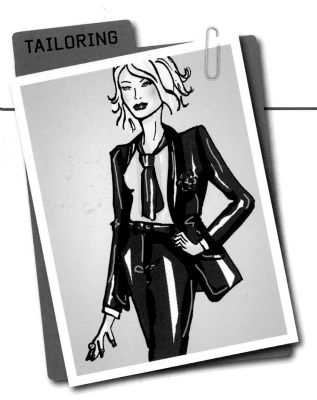

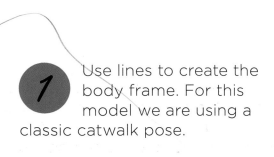

1 Use lines to create the body frame. For this model we are using a classic catwalk pose.

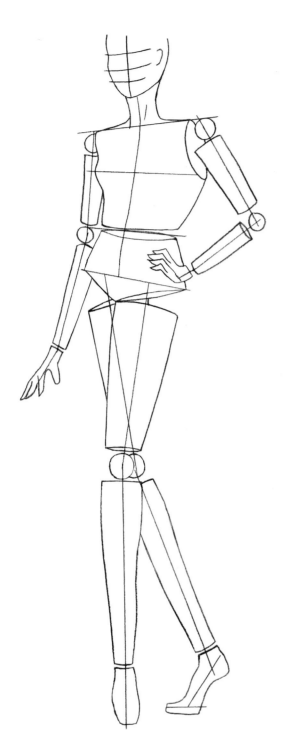

2 Build your frame using your basic shapes. Put the back leg behind the body to balance the bent elbow on the arm above.

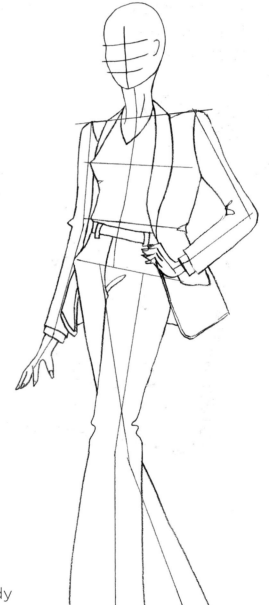

3 Now draw the outfit onto your body frame. Flare the jacket out behind the hand on the hip to show the tailored shape. Add the stiletto shoes to give the model height, which will also make the trousers look longer.

4 Remove the frame and add the facial features and hair style. To keep the look soft and feminine, a loose relaxed hairstyle is used.

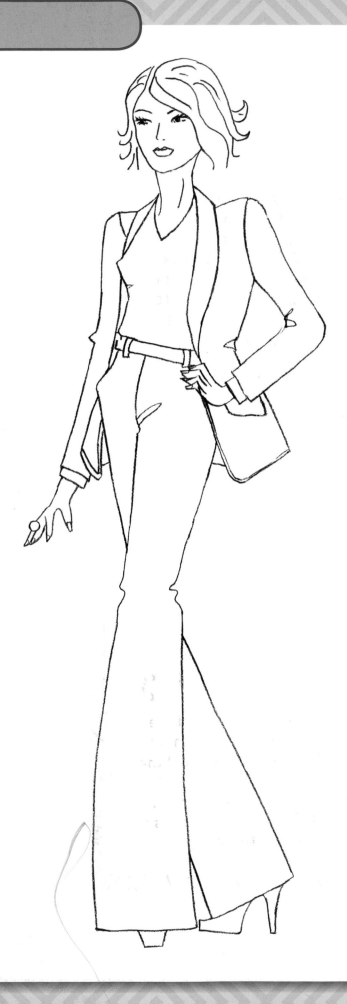

5 Make sure you are really happy with your pencil line before going to ink. Check that your facial features and hairstyle are soft enough to balance out the masculine styling of the suit.

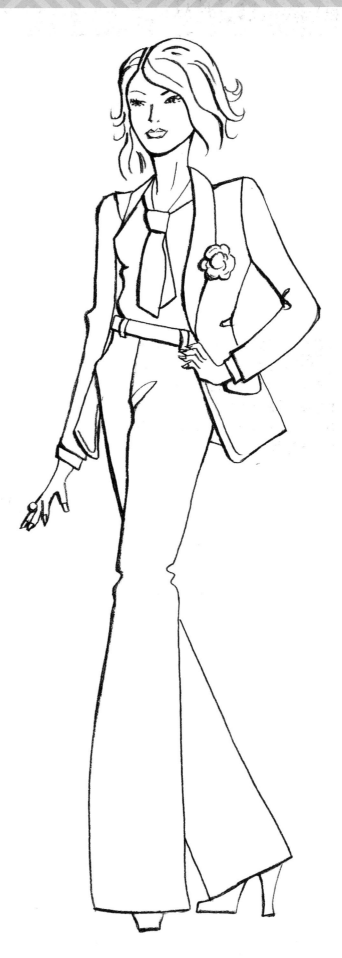

Add an Accessory

Now it's time to add the accessories. Put a short feature neck tie around the model's neck, along with a flower on the jacket lapel. A matching dress ring adds a feminine touch.

6 Use your finished pencil to start working up your ink. Add the thicker lines around the opening of the jacket and down the top of the trouser legs. Thicker lines used around the neck tie and flower will really make them stand out as features.

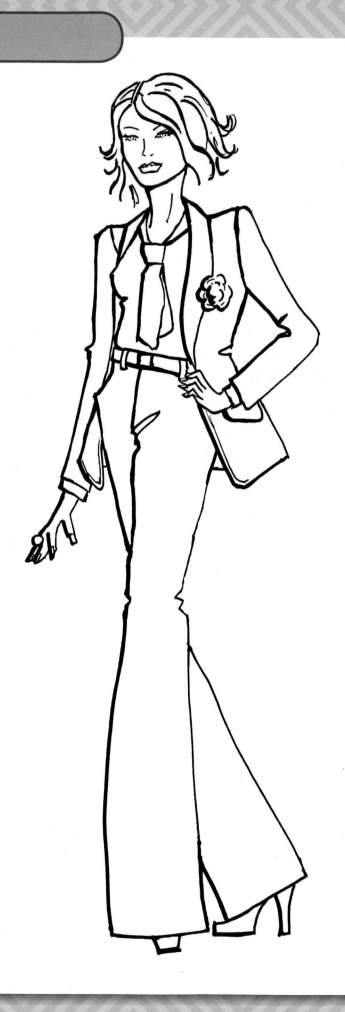

Stylist's tip

When inking the lines of your flower, take inspiration from nature. Look at images of real flowers, as well as fabric corsages, to help get the detail right.

7 Use dark blue on the suit, highlighted with a sky blue shirt. Contrast with a fuchsia pink tie and belt to really make this outfit stand out. Add complementary make up to the model's face and finish off with light blonde hair.

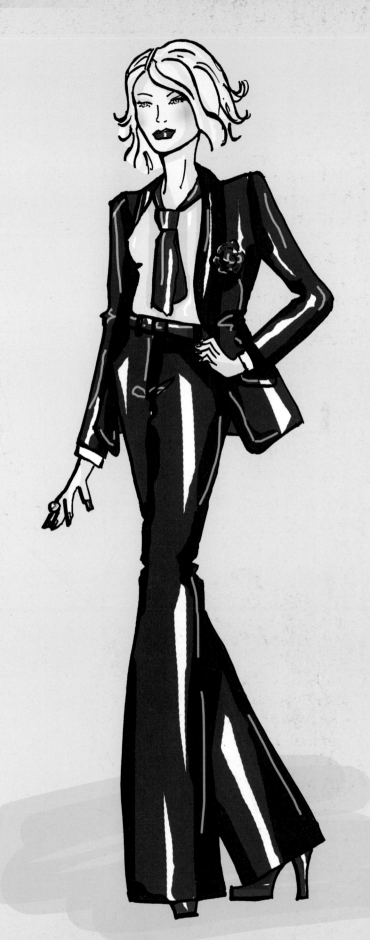

Alexander McQueen

Sarah Burton designed this wedding dress and worked with the Royal School of Needlework to create an elegant, timeless and stunning piece. It's perfect for a princess and every girl's dream wedding day.

COUTURE

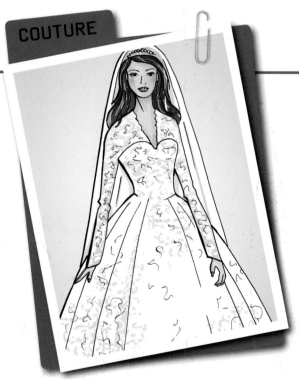

1 Pencil in your pose. A simple elegant but girly pose works well with this statement dress. Keep the arms and legs at soft angles.

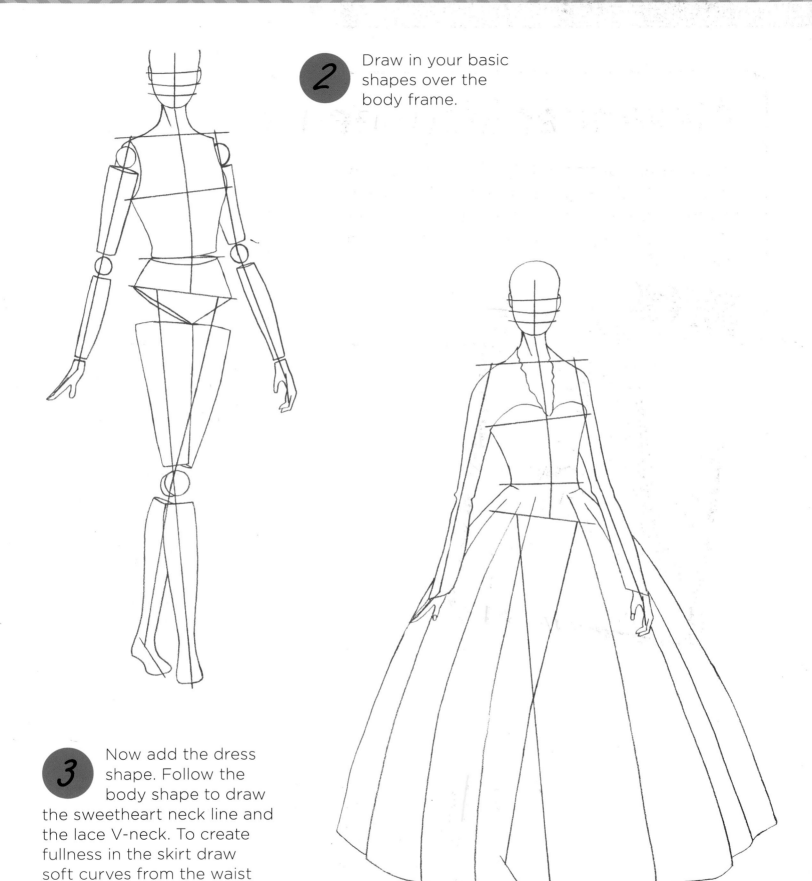

2 Draw in your basic shapes over the body frame.

3 Now add the dress shape. Follow the body shape to draw the sweetheart neck line and the lace V-neck. To create fullness in the skirt draw soft curves from the waist through to the hem.

4 For the model's hairstyle a gentle wave works well, which will sit smoothly behind the shoulders. Add the facial features, keeping the face looking straight forward to give the model an elegant feel.

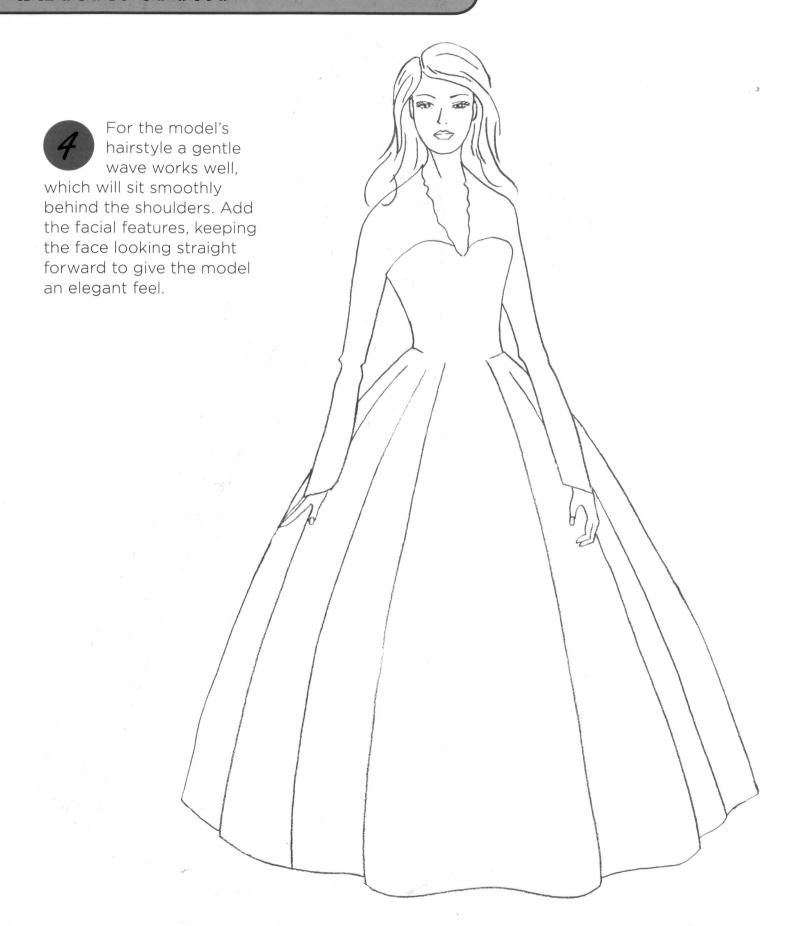

5 Draw in your lace detail using a light pencil. Start a little heavier at the top, then lighter and less consistent down through the skirt. Draw in the veil by following the lines of the arms. Top off with a delicate tiara and matching earrings.

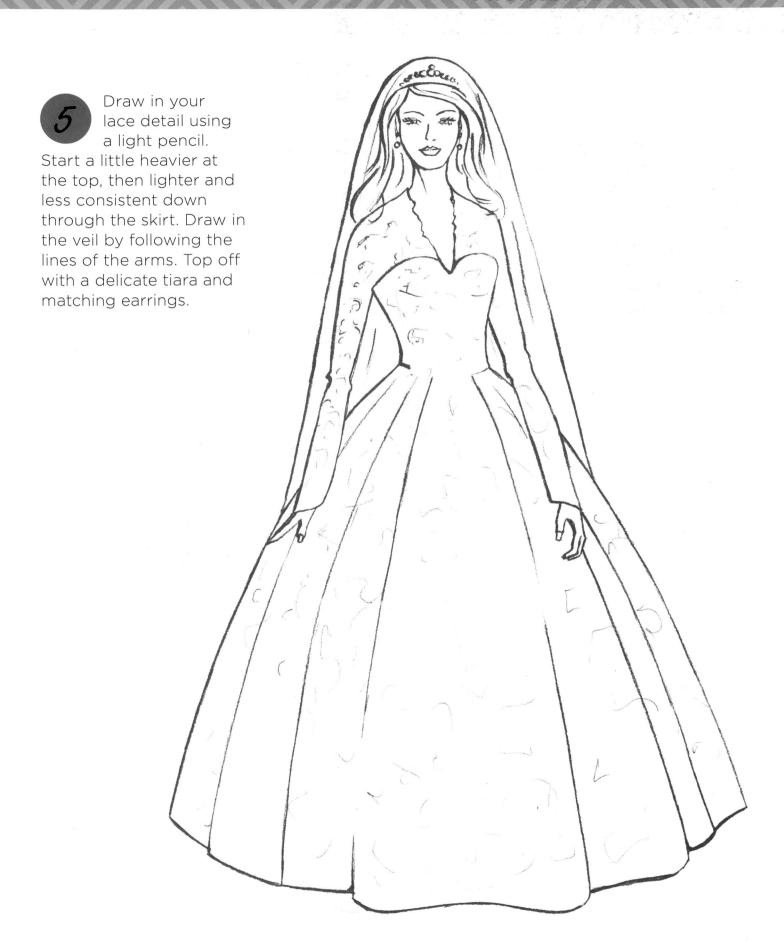

6 Start working up your pencil with ink. Use a light, thin pen for the lace detail throughout the dress. Add heavier lines to the base of the dress, arms and around the waist. Also, add thicker lines through the hair to help it stand out against the veil.

Stylist's tip

Look at different types of lace so you can see the different effects it has over other fabrics and against your own skin.

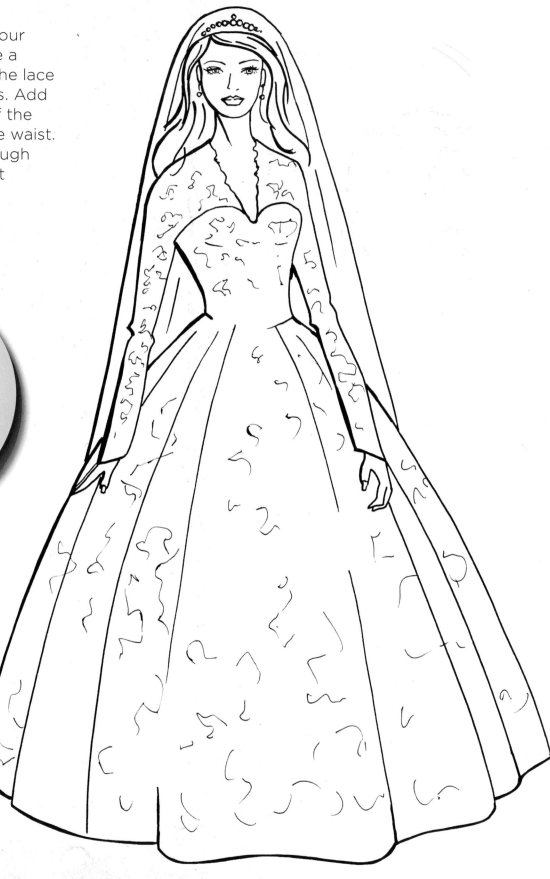

7 White is the colour used throughout this stunning dress. Use touches of grey to show shades of the lace detail. For the lace on the arms, use white in various places so the skin colour shows through. This will make the lace look light and fresh against the skin.

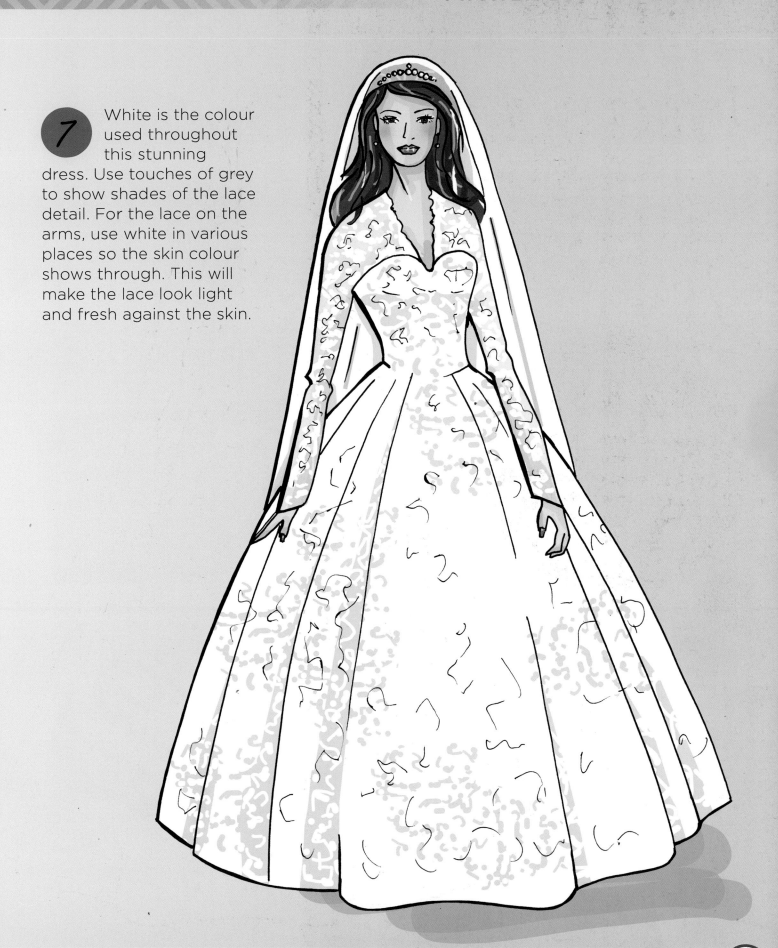

STYLE CARDS

Classic, simple, fun or just plain eccentric – fashion designers are 'out there' and we love them for it. With their wonderful range of fashion accessories Chanel, Dior, Gucci and Prada have proved that they can stand the test of time. They also know how to make you feel truly special.

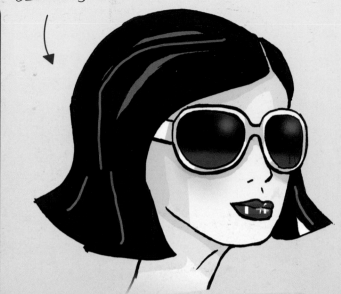

Prada sunglasses for scorching summer days.

CHANEL:

Coco Chanel was probably one of the most iconic designers. Mixing elegance, sophistication and originality, her style is timeless and still influencing the catwalk.

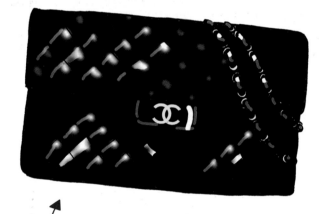

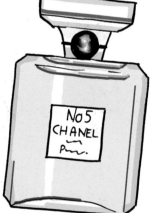

Made famous by Marilyn Monroe, this perfume is a must have on any girl's dressing table.

No 5 CHANEL

Quilted handbag, perfect for dressing up an outfit.

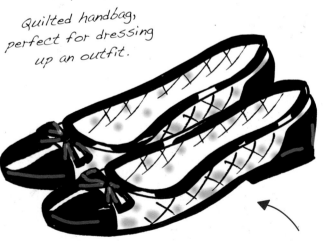

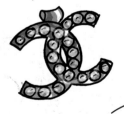

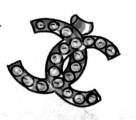

Unmistakable Chanel logo diamond studded earrings.

These simple black and white pumps are enhanced by the Chanel use of quilting.

French nail polish is sophisticated and elegant.

SHOES:

You can't finish off a designer outfit without designer shoes. There are lots out there to choose from. Here are a couple of dazzling pairs.

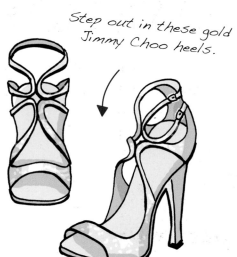

Blue satin Manolos finish off a classy outfit beautifully.

Step out in these gold Jimmy Choo heels.

SCARFS:

Scarfs are a cheap and easy way to add the designer look to any outfit.

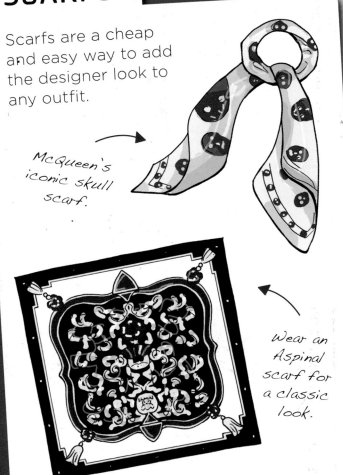

McQueen's iconic skull scarf.

Wear an Aspinal scarf for a classic look.

BAGS:

One of the key designer accessories is the handbag. It can be simple and subtle or decorated with designer logos.

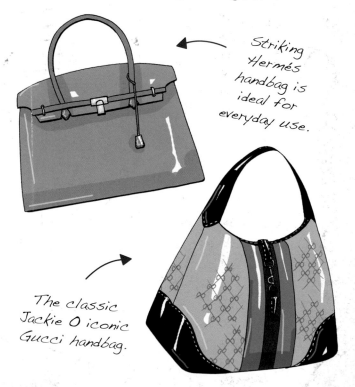

Striking Hermés handbag is ideal for everyday use.

The classic Jackie O iconic Gucci handbag.

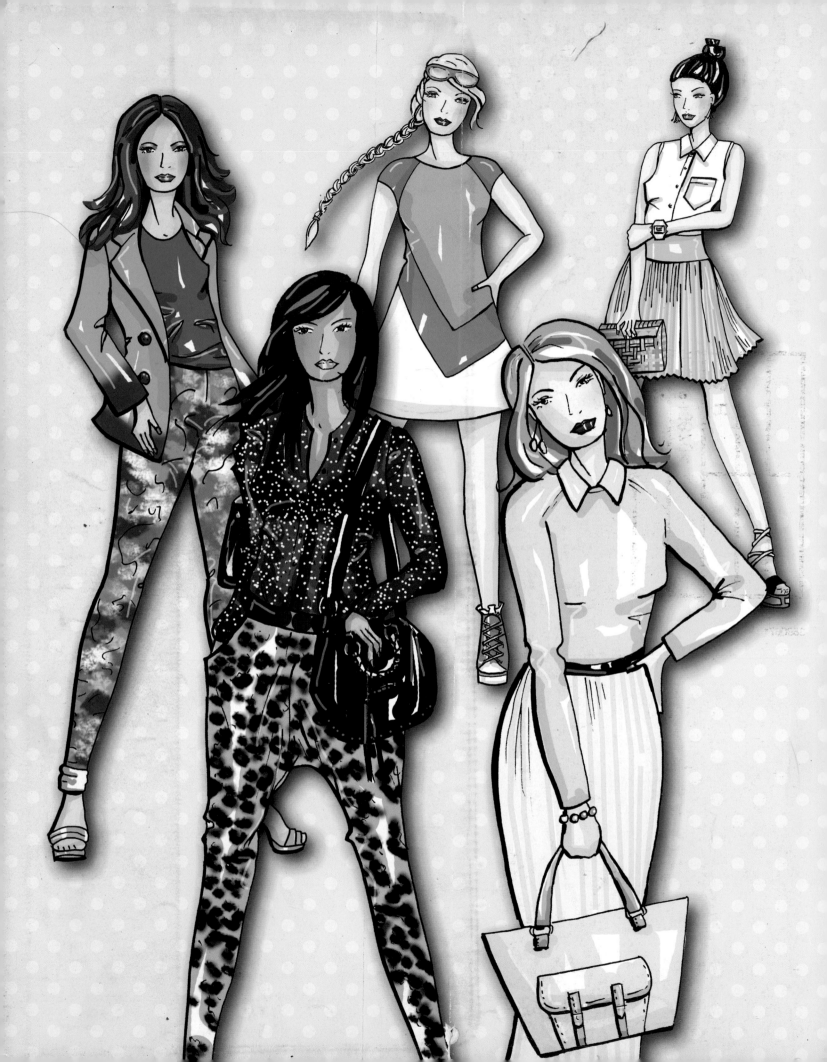